DOG TALES

To David —

Warm Regards
+
all the best!

Ray McSorley

+

Jake 🐾

January '92

DOG TALES

HOW TO SOLVE THE MOST TROUBLESOME BEHAVIOR PROBLEMS OF MAN'S BEST FRIEND

Ray McSoley

WITH LARRY ROTHSTEIN

WARNER BOOKS

A Warner Communications Company

Warner Books, Inc., 666 Fifth Avenue, New York, NY 10103

 A Warner Communications Company

Printed in the United States of America

First Printing: March 1988

10 9 8 7 6 5 4 3 2 1

Library of Congress Cataloging-in-Publication Data

McSoley, Ray.
  Dog tales.

  1. Dogs. 2. Dogs—Training. I. Rothstein, Larry.
II. Title.
SF426.2.M385 1988   636.7   87-40419
ISBN 0-446-51353-9

Photographs by Janet Knott

Book design by H. Roberts

D E D I C A T I O N

To my wife, Mary, for loving a man she knows marches to a different drummer.

And to Michael, Kristen and Marianne, I love you all.

C O N T E N T S

ACKNOWLEDGMENTS / ix
FOREWORD / xi
INTRODUCTION / 1

SECTION I
CHAPTER 1: *Ray's Rules* / **9**
CHAPTER 2: *Ray's Questions* / **17**
CHAPTER 3: *Structure: The Five Basic Commands* / **25**
CHAPTER 4: *Simple Reinforcement: Avoidance Collar* / **43**
CHAPTER 5: *Advanced Reinforcement: Electric Collar* / **51**

SECTION II
CHAPTER 6: *Aggressive Behavior* / **59**
CHAPTER 7: *Housesoiling* / **75**
CHAPTER 8: *Phobias* / **87**
CHAPTER 9: *Destructive Behavior* / **99**
CHAPTER 10: *Barking* / **109**
CHAPTER 11: *Disobedience* / **117**

SECTION III

CHAPTER 12: *Puppies* / **131**
CHAPTER 13: *Older Dogs* / **157**
CHAPTER 14: *Children* / **161**
CHAPTER 15: *Just for the Fun of It* / **169**
APPENDIX / **173**

ACKNOWLEDGMENTS

Almost two years ago I received a telephone call from Larry Rothstein, who had read an article about me by Nina McCann in the Boston *Globe*. He asked me if I had an interest in writing a book. That was the beginning of *Dog Tales*. My work with dogs, however, began long before that call, starting with my own Labrador retrievers. I was given unknown assistance by William Campbell, whose book peaked my interest in canine problem behavior. Although we've yet to meet, thanks, Bill. To Katherine A. Houpt, V.M.D.Ph.D., of Cornell University, thank you for sharing your knowledge. Thanks also to the veterinarians, technicians and receptionists who, over the years, have provided me with a steady stream of clients. My sincere thanks also to the entire staff of the Angell Memorial Animal Hospital for making me feel at home on Tuesdays and special thanks go to Gus W. Thornton, D.V.M., for bringing me aboard.

To the Acorn Animal Hospital; Ashdod Animal Hospital; Bellingham Veterinary Clinic; Belmont Animal Hospital; Bay State Animal Clinic; Brookline Animal Hospital; Cape Ann Veterinary Hospital; Carlisle Animal Hospital; Chabot Veterinary Hospital; Commonwealth Veterinary Clinic; Dr. Wolf's Animal Hospital; Dr. Zullo's Natick Animal Hospital; Driftway Animal Hospital; Duxbury Animal Hospital; Concord Animal Hospital; Fanning Veterinary Clinic; Fresh Pond Animal Hospital; Framingham Animal Hospital; Heritage Hill Veterinary Clinic; Hingham Animal

Clinic; Hudson Animal Hospital; Kingston Animal Hospital; Linwood Animal Hospital; William Looby, D.V.M.; Richard Cohen, V.M.D.; Lexington-Bedford Veterinary Hospital; Main Street Veterinary Clinic; Marlboro Animal Hospital; Medway Animal Hospital; Morrissey Animal Hospital; New England Veterinary Clinic; Slade Veterinarian Clinic; Oak Hill Animal Hospital; Rotherwood Animal Clinic; Roberts Animal Hospital; No. Main St. Veterinary Clinic; McGrath Animal Hospital; Saugus Animal Hospital; Sharon Veterinary Clinic; Silver Lake Veterinary Hospital, Stow Animal Hospital; Windhover Bird Clinic; Westbridge Veterinary Hospital; Wayland Animal Clinic; West Roxbury Animal Hospital, Inc.; Weston Veterinary Clinic; Westboro Animal Hospital; Watertown Animal Hospital; Westwood Animal Hospital, more thanks than I can ever repay!

To all the groomers, trainers, and kennel owners who have helped me, thank you. Thanks also to the many breeders who, over the years, have taught me so much.

I want to thank my agent, Helen Rees, for getting things rolling. To all the people at Warner Books who were involved, thank you. Special thanks to Jamie Raab and Jamie Rothstein, whose steady hands on the tiller and heavy red pencil improved much of the book. I cannot thank Larry Rothstein properly. I can merely say, "Thanks, Larry," for your support, your patience, and most of all, for your search for excellence with this book. To Ken Rivard, thank you.

To all those clients who offered their dogs for pictures, to Mr. and Mrs. Charles Sarkis who graciously provided the setting, to Janet Knott, whose superb talent with a camera provided the photographs, many many thanks, and to Dan Jones for pitching in. Lastly, to my clients, thank you. Dog owners are truly special people. And they all cared enough for their pets to seek help for them when they were in trouble. My finest teachers have been the dogs themselves. From them I have learned far more than how and why they behave as they do. I have learned patience and humility. I have learned how to be a good listener and observer. And finally, I have learned that they are, indeed, man's best friend.

F O R E W O R D

Dog Tales is a book that a wide range of dog owners will find both enjoyable and informative. In additional to dog owners whose pets have behaviorial problems, anyone contemplating dog ownership or anyone who wishes to avoid behavior problems will also profit from reading this book.

Drawing on his vast experience and using actual case studies, Ray McSoley makes behaviorial problems, their causes and the action needed to alter them come to life. The combination of this expertise and the case study format allows the reader to easily follow the author through the detection, correction and follow-up prevention of behaviorial problems in dogs.

I have known Ray McSoley for a number of years. He initially made an appointment with me to discuss the possibility of being affiliated with the veterinary staff of the MSPCA's Angell Memorial Animal Hospital. As he discussed his desire to broaden his capability of providing assistance to owners with pets that have behavioral problems and to veterinarians who have clients seeking advice on everything from simple house training techniques to severe behavior problems, the possibility of having him affiliated with the Hospital became very exciting. The affiliation over the years has been just that.

Veterinarians are frequently asked for guidance on behavioral problems and, in many instances, feel uncomfortable or not adequately informed to give complete and accurate advice. Having the services of Ray McSoley to refer clients to has been extremely helpful to members of our staff, our patients and pet owners. I know that veterinarians at many other hospitals have had the same experience.

Over the years, I have referred many clients to him. I would characterize Ray McSoley as competent, kind, patient, thorough, fair and realistic. He always is willing to take the time required to analyze carefully a behavioral problem. He is thorough in providing information about the problem, its likely causes and clear instructions for correcting it to the owner. He is patient and supportive during the sometimes long and difficult process of correction. Finally, he is not afraid to admit that some problems are so serious and major, that they can't be solved. These same characteristics of the man and his method of working with owners and pets, comes through in the pages of Dog Tales.

Gus W. Thornton, D.V.M.
Chief of Staff
Angell Memorial Hospital

DOG TALES

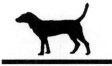

Introduction

I LOVE dogs.

That might seem like an obvious statement from someone who has spent the last twelve years traveling around New England dealing with dog problems. But my love for dogs has been tested over and over again in my visits. I've been badly bitten, and scratched. I've seen dogs that have had an entire household in anguish and a neighborhood in fear.

I've entered these situations with one goal in mind: to help the animal and his owners establish a happy and loving relationship. In most cases I've succeeded. No matter how difficult the case, I've usually showed owners how to eliminate their dog problems by using the powerful set of techniques I've developed over the years.

I've been asked many times why I took up such an unusual profession where I pile up forty thousand miles a year on the road. The reason is simple: I've always wanted to do something that helped people. I get a special feeling when after a few visits I see real progress, a healthy relationship between owner and dog developing, a seemingly intractable problem cured.

Yet, in my visits I'm continually astonished at how

little owners know about the cause of their dogs' behavior problems or how to deal with them. What they have read, seen or heard has not worked. Many owners have completely altered their lives in order to accommodate their dogs. Owners come up with crazy solutions because they don't have any idea what to do—they think they have dog problems because they're bad owners or they have a bad dog or they used a bad trainer. Usually this isn't true. What they need are new ways of thinking about their problems and creative ideas on how to solve them. That is why I've written this book.

My clients have found my methods practical and easy to master. Some of my techniques are highly innovative, while others are variations of more conventional approaches. Some deal directly with the dog, while most involve changing the interaction between owner and dog.

I must confess that until shortly before I decided to become a dog analyst I understood as little about these animals as do most of my clients. My ideas and feelings were rooted in my own limited—but largely happy—experience. Only when I ran into problems with one of my dogs did I start to question what I was doing.

I was seven years old when my love affair with dogs began. Every summer my father, who managed the Hotel Statler in Cleveland, would bring the family to Manomet, Massachusetts. In my fourth year in Manomet, I met a gigantic black Labrador retriever named Smokey, who lived a few houses down the road. Smokey was a great dog— energetic, friendly and lots of fun. He soon became a member of our family, arriving every Saturday morning for breakfast, waiting patiently by the wood-burning stove for my mother to give him the leftover bacon, eggs, and popovers she'd prepared for us. He'd gulp down these culinary delights and then bark for me to take him on a run. Sprinting out the door, we'd be off for a day-long adventure.

I had the pleasure of knowing Smokey for four years. When I was eleven his owners didn't return to Manomet. I never saw Smokey again.

My next experience with a dog wasn't as pleasant. A friend of my mother gave her a black American cocker spaniel puppy named Mike as a birthday present. Unfortunately, Mike had the personality of a four-legged Attila the Hun. Whenever my dad tried to discipline him he'd growl and show his teeth. Mike and I never had any major problems —after a couple of difficult encounters with Mike I made up my mind to stay clear of him.

It wasn't until I finished college in Boston and was married that I had my own dog. After my wife, Mary, and I bought our first home I acquired a black Lab named Licorice, who was a fine dog. Unfortunately, she died when she was three. I continued my love affair with Labs when I bought Kate, a yellow Lab, who was as wonderful a dog as Smokey had been. She had an easygoing personality that was perfect for the three children Mary and I were raising. Like most owners who have no problems with their dogs, I was just plain lucky.

But I got my comeuppance with my next dog, Geordy (pronounced Jeordy), a handsome, ninety-five pound black Lab who was very resistant to training. Unless I constantly worked with Geordy I'd lose control. For example, I could get Geordy to heel if I worked with him every day, but if I slacked off for a week, Geordy would drag me up and down the street. Geordy perplexed me. Why couldn't I control him? My career as a dog analyst—though unknown to me—was about to begin.

My first step on the road to my new career began when I started doing a little detective work, talking to my breeder, Jean Young, about Geordy's behavior as a puppy. Jean reminded me that she had recommended another, more passive dog. I was the one who couldn't resist Geordy because he was so energetic. I realized that I had unknowingly let myself in for the problems I was having.

My second step was to start thinking about how to move beyond the standard techniques for training a dog to heel. The way I'd been taught was that if the dog ran out in front you drag him back to you. Geordy almost seemed to laugh at this method. I fiddled around with a variety of approaches to heeling until I found one that I thought would work (you'll read about this later in the book). My third step was to try it out on Geordy. Slowly, after a lot of hard work, I got Geordy to heel correctly. I then started playing around with the other standard commands—sit, stay, down, coming when called—to gain more control over Geordy. They worked nicely and his resistence started to subside. I finally began to enjoy this handsome fellow.

All this was amateur work though. I never dreamed that shortly I'd be doing it to earn a living.

By age thirty-five I was suffering from career burnout. I had risen to the vice presidency of a major truck leasing firm, but I no longer wanted to climb the corporate ladder. I was desperately unhappy. With Mary's support, I decided to take a couple of months off to figure out what I wanted to do. I didn't realize how quickly I'd find the answer.

During the third week of my self-imposed sabbatical I received a telephone call from Jean Young, who wanted to know if I was interested in acquiring a two-year-old male yellow Labrador.

"Jean," I said in all seriousness, thinking about Kate and Geordy, "if I take another dog, you'd better open up your guest room, because Mary will throw me out on my ear." I then told her about my leaving my job. Jean, an ebullient woman, as understanding of people as she is of dogs, said, "Well, Ray, with all the time you have on your hands, why don't you call up Mrs. Johnson and see if you could help her with her yellow lab."

Jean went on to explain that Mrs. Johnson, who was in her mid-fifties, had lived alone with her dog Simba since her husband died. Mrs. Johnson felt she could no longer keep her dog because he was out of control. Jean thought I might show Mrs. Johnson how to handle Simba because of what I had achieved with Geordy. I told Jean I'd be willing to try and called Mrs. Johnson that day to set up an appointment for the next morning.

Mrs. Johnson started crying when she told me why she had to give up Simba. "Mr. McSoley, I'm just not strong enough to handle him. I brought him to obedience school and I still can't manage him. I don't know what else to do but give him away."

I looked at Simba, who was calmly sitting in the corner

of the living room watching us talk. He didn't seem to be a particularly active dog. I thought he could quickly be brought under control if Mrs. Johnson would agree to follow what I had learned from Geordy. I told Mrs. Johnson I was convinced she could keep Simba by using some of the techniques I had developed. I explained how I wanted to approach the problem—I'd teach her the basic structuring commands using the variations I'd developed (which are fully described further on in this book).

Mrs. Johnson thought carefully for a moment and then said, "Mr. McSoley, let's give it a try. I'll do anything to keep Simba."

Thus the career of Ray McSoley, animal behavioral therapist, was launched. After five sessions I had Mrs. Johnson and Simba working together beautifully. And I can't tell you the pride I felt when I watched Mrs. Johnson and Simba heeling perfectly as they walked the quiet streets of Dover, Massachusetts.

The next boost toward my new career came from Mrs. Johnson's veterinarian, who was so impressed with Simba's new manners that he called me and asked if I'd get in touch with a couple of his patients who were having a hard time with their dogs. I quickly agreed to pay them a visit.

I saw these patients' dogs and had as easy a time getting them under control as I had with Simba. Four more vets called to refer their patients' dog problems to me. I suddenly began to believe I might actually make a living at being a Jim Rockford for dog owners. I began calling local veterinarians for referrals and read every book I could get my hands on relating to dog problems and dog behavior.

One thing I was convinced of almost immediately—I had to visit people in their homes and watch how they dealt with their dog. The interaction between owner and pet was the key to unlocking the trouble. That's why most dog training failed—it couldn't be translated into the home environment. And I kept trying different, imaginative ways to deal with particular problems. What methods worked I kept, what didn't I threw out.

This is what this book is all about—the theories and

methods I use to solve dog problems and the stories of the people and dogs I have encountered over the last twelve years.

I've designed this book to re-create the way I work with owners to help them with their pups. I want you to feel that I am sitting in your kitchen listening to you tell me about your dog problems. After reading this book, you should be able not only to recognize your own dog's problems, but to solve them as well.

To this end, I've divided the book into three major sections. In the first section, I provide you with all the major tools and information that you will need to deal with your dog problems and establish a healthy relationship with your dog. In the second section, we'll look at the major problems owners face—aggression, destructive behavior, barking, phobias—through the cases I have been brought in to solve. In Section Three, we'll examine the best way to prevent these problems from occurring—by properly raising puppies and integrating older dogs into the home, and how your children should interact with your pet.

Finally, I'd like to say that if after a long, weary day of crisscrossing New England visiting dog owners I ever wonder whether I made the right choice taking up the rather strange career of a consulting dog analyst, I've only to think of the thousands of healthy and happy relationships I have helped start, and my doubts disappear. My hope is that this book will continue the work that is my living and my joy.

SECTION
I

CHAPTER

1

Ray's Rules

W HEN I begin a case I tell clients about my seven rules for dog ownership, which I believe every owner has to understand and follow. Let's look at why these rules are so necessary.

Charlie Rivard; a young architect who lived alone in a third-floor walk-up in the elegant Back Bay section of Boston. Charlie called me because he felt that he had little control over his golden retriever, Dixie. As Charlie and I sat in his kitchen talking about his problems, Dixie ran in from the living room and jumped up on Charlie, who pushed his dog away, saying, "Dixie, go to your bed." The dog retreated to a corner, curling onto the blue blanket that was his bed.

Charlie grinned, obviously pleased that he had gotten Dixie to obey. Charlie and I resumed our discussion, but several minutes later, Dixie got up from his blanket, walked over to Charlie and jumped up again. Charlie grabbed the dog by the collar and dragged him back to his bed shouting, "Now stay there, you damn dog."

I'm sure you've guessed what happened next. A couple of minutes later, Dixie left his bed again and raced toward Charlie, who repeated dragging him back to his bed. Charlie looked at me and said, "See what I mean, he's a stupid, damn dog. He doesn't understand one thing I tell him."

"Charlie," I asked. "What do you want him to do?"

"I want the dog to stay in his bed."

"Well then," I replied. "Do you ever praise him when he's lying in his bed?"

That pulled Charlie up short. He stopped, thought about it for a few seconds, and said, "No, I guess I never do."

I explained to Charlie that what he was really communicating to Dixie was that every time he wanted attention all he had to do was leave the corner and come over to Charlie. Charlie thought he was telling him to go away because that's what his words said. But Dixie didn't speak English. All he understood was that he was rewarded for coming over.

Charlie looked stunned.

I continued. "If you want Dixie to stay in his bed, then bring him to his spot, tie him with a short line to the baseboard and say, 'Good dog.'" I told Charlie to then go and sit in his chair. "When the dog calms down, periodically turn and say in a pleasant voice, 'Good dog. Good dog.'" I wanted him to reinforce the correct behavior. This way Charlie rewarded Dixie for doing the right thing, rather than punished him for doing the wrong thing. *You can never teach the correct behavior by merely punishing the incorrect behavior.*

Charlie, of course, had to restructure his entire relationship with Dixie before he could gain complete control over his dog. But Charlie had to understand *he was communicating exactly the wrong thing.* Like many owners, Charlie was unknowingly reinforcing the very behavior he didn't want.

Here's another example of miscommunication. Every time a thunderstorm passed by Patti Levy's dog Slater became anxious and trembled violently. What did Patti do? Like many owners she called her dog over, patted her on the head and said, "That's okay. Don't be afraid. That's a good girl." What was she trying to do? Reassure the dog. What did the dog understand? "I guess my owner likes me to tremble. She's patting me on the head. I think I'll tremble some more." Instead of curtailing her dog's trembling, Patti ended up encouraging it without realizing what she was doing.

A final story. When Steve Williams returned home from work one day, his puppy raced to the front door and became so excited he urinated on the living room floor. Many puppies do this. But Steve didn't understand this. He yelled at the pup, "Bad dog, bad dog" and whacked him across the rear. Pushing the dog's face into the urine, he shouted, "Don't you ever do that again!"

The next day when Steve came home from work, what do you think happened? As soon as he stepped through the door the puppy peed on the floor. Steve couldn't believe it! This time he gave the puppy two resounding smacks on his rear. That should do the trick, Steve thought as he went off to prepare supper. What he didn't realize was that he was conditioning fear in the puppy.

The next night the puppy urinated again and Steve hit the puppy again. Williams was well on his way to having a puppy who will continue to urinate whenever Steve walks through the door.

These examples all point out rule number one: YOU MUST BE RESPONSIBLE FOR LEARNING HOW TO COMMUNICATE WITH YOUR DOG. I've seen thousands of owners reinforcing behaviors they don't want. Invariably, miscommunication stems from owners not understanding what the dog is thinking. You must learn to think like your dog and stop projecting human responses onto the animal.

This brings us to my second rule. In the above stories the owners weren't controlling the relationship. The fundamental fact that must be communicated to your dog is that YOU MUST BE THE LEADER AND THE DOG MUST BE THE FOLLOWER—THERE'S NO ROOM FOR EQUALITY IN THE DOG'S MIND. You can't simply be a buddy with your dog, or it leads to disaster. The dog must be— and wants to be—subordinate to your wishes.

The reason for this lies in the nature of dogs. Dogs are descendants of wolves, who live in packs. Every pack has what animal scientists call an alpha wolf, who runs the pack and establishes order and peace. From him other wolves learn their place in the pack hierarchy.

Dogs are like wolves in that if the owner is not going to run the relationship—be the alpha dog—then the dog will. He needs order and will impose his own if his owner won't. As we'll see in later chapters, once the dog is in charge a host of behavioral problems can result.

Remember it's unnatural for the dog to exist in an equal relationship. Dogs, like children, are happiest when they know their place, their limits and their role. They look to you for leadership and you must provide it.

When I tell my clients this they look embarrassed. "But Mr. McSoley," they say, "Bozo's my pal, I don't want to be his boss." Or they admit candidly, "I don't have a dominant personality." I tell my clients that they don't have to change themselves into George Patton to gain control. My program can be implemented by anyone, no matter how mild-mannered.

My third rule is that IF YOU'RE NOT TEACHING YOUR DOG THE RIGHT BEHAVIOR, YOU'RE TEACHING HIM THE WRONG BEHAVIOR—BECAUSE YOU'RE ALWAYS TEACHING HIM SOMETHING. For example, you're sitting in your living room reading the paper. Bozo comes over, nudges you under the arm, and grabs the bottom of *The Daily Planet* with his teeth. Distractedly you say, "Go away, boy" and push him away with the paper. Bozo really sinks his teeth into your paper and you start a tug-of-war game. Although a part of you is upset, a part of you is enjoying playing the game. Finally, you get tired and grab Bozo by the collar and drag him into the kitchen, informing him in no uncertain terms to leave you alone. What have you just taught your dog? First that tug-of-war is all right. And second that every time he wants to play, you will too. Do you realize you're encouraging this behavior? No, of course not. You think you're getting rid of the dog. But what you're really doing is teaching the dog that he's the leader of the relationship.

Rule number four flows logically from rule three: YOU MUST BE CONSISTENT IN DEALING WITH YOUR DOG.

Most owners don't realize how inconsistent they are. I ask an owner, "Do you feed your dog from the table?" The owner shakes her head, "No, I never do." "Never?" I ask again. "Not normally." She pauses. "Well, for special occasions—his birthday, maybe my birthday." "Is that all?" "Well, Christmas and Thanksgiving, the holidays . . . you know."

Small inconsistencies are usually the tip of the iceberg. As I continue my questioning and observations I soon discover many inconsistencies between what the owner says she is doing and what she really is doing. I also begin to pick up the inconsistencies between the way the owner deals with the dog and the way other members of the family deal with the dog. For example, an owner may have trained her dog to sit quietly while the family is eating supper. But her children undermine her efforts by giving food to the dog under the table. Or she finds her husband punishing her dog after she has established a good program of control through positive rewards. Such inconsistencies must stop if a proper relationship is to be established.

Rule number five is very important for owners to understand but most have a great deal of difficulty with it. DON'T EXPECT YOUR DOG TO KNOW THE DIFFERENCE BETWEEN RIGHT AND WRONG—HE'S NOT A LITTLE PERSON IN A FUR COAT.

Most owners won't buy this. "Ray," they insist, "Bozo peed on the rug because he was getting back at me." Do you mean he was spiteful, I ask. "Yes, of course he was. He was angry with me."

No he wasn't.

Owners think dogs are angry or spiteful because of the desire to project human characteristics onto dogs. We've all been brought up with images of *Lady and the Tramp*, Snoopy, Lassie, Rin Tin Tin, Huckleberry Hound—where dogs either talk or act like human beings. We *want* them to act like human beings, because they're more fun and charming when we think of them that way. But reality is quite different.

Here's a specific case. A young woman named Lois Gantz left her house and returned several hours later. When Lois walked through the door she saw that her couch had been shredded. At this exact moment, Chala, her Shih Tzu, sauntered in and spotted her mistress turning nine shades of purple. Chala's ears went back, her head went down, and her rear hit the floor. Lois thought Chala was expressing guilt, and started to chase her dog so she could whack the stuffing out of her.

Unfortunately, Lois had completely misunderstood what she had just seen. Chala had no idea what Lois was mad about. Chala ripped up the couch hours ago, and made no connection between that activity and Lois's rage. Furthermore, while Chala was clawing at the couch she didn't think she was doing anything bad.

What Lois didn't understand was that her beloved Shih Tzu was behaving in a submissive manner because she saw Lois's angry face. Chala knew from past situations that when Lois's face becomes distorted and her voice gets angry she is about to be punished. Chala thought, "Oh boy, what happened now, I'm in trouble. I better get out of here." All Lois was doing was making herself feel better by letting out her anger.

This leads me to rule number six: YOU MUST BE CERTAIN YOUR DOG UNDERSTANDS WHY HE'S BEING CORRECTED. In the above example, Chala doesn't know why Lois is angry with her. What Lois has to do is set up a program of conditioning Chala toward proper behavior. Within this program correction and punishment have a context and can be used effectively. I'll explain this program in detail in later chapters, but for now, simply remember this rule.

The corollary of this principle is rule number seven: REWARD YOUR DOG FOR THE PROPER BEHAVIOR. This is the key concept behind any successful program of dealing with dog problems. Owners have to get away from punishment and work with the dog in a positive way. You have to get used to saying "Good dog" when your dog sits, stays, comes when called, and heels correctly. Your dog loves to hear these words and will work hard to please you.

These seven rules are the cornerstones of a good relationship with your dog. We'll see their importance repeatedly in the cases that follow and by the end of the book you will understand the full significance of each one. The rules are again:

RAY'S RULES

1. You must be responsible for learning how to communicate with your dog.
2. You must be the leader and the dog must be the follower—there's no room for equality in the dog's mind.
3. If you're not teaching your dog the right behavior, you're teaching him the wrong behavior—because you're always teaching him something.
4. You must be consistent in dealing with your dog.
5. Don't expect your dog to know the difference between right and wrong—he's not a little person in a fur coat.
6. You must be certain your dog understands why he's being corrected.
7. Reward your dog for the proper behavior.

CHAPTER
2

Ray's Questions

T HE speed with which I grasp the nature of most dog problems often astonishes my clients. What they don't realize is that the information leading to my insights is right in front of them too—if they only knew how to look for it.

I always begin my analysis with a series of questions that helps me identify the problem, decide how the dog should change his behavior, determine how the owner must change his or her behavior, and specify the specific steps necessary for developing a proper relationship.

My questions cover the following areas:

- The history of the dog
- What the owner thinks the dog's problem is
- The dog's behavior outside the house
- The dog's behavior with others
- How the dog obeys
- Health problems and dietary information

In each area I ask very specific questions—how much, how long, when, with whom, how many times, and so forth. I want to know exactly what the dog is doing and exactly what the owner and other people in contact with the dog are doing. By prodding owners to be specific I get a clear picture of the dog's problem and the relationship between owner and dog. Furthermore, as owners answer these questions and think about exactly what their dog is doing, they become more objective about their predicament. My questions put a little distance between them and the emotions of the moment.

At first most owners have difficulty being specific. Their memories aren't good, and they often describe events and problems in vague terms. Frequently they say something like, "I don't understand it, Bozo was such a pleasant dog and one day he just took a bite out of the postman's pants." Or just as common is, "I don't know what's the matter with him, maybe he's just moody."

Those statements aren't helpful to me or to you as you think about how to correct your dog problem. You have to know *specifically* what happened and how it happened.

This chapter provides the questions I use in each interview. Ask these questions about your own situation, and have family members and friends help you respond. I've also included a questionnaire form for you to fill out when you work on your dog problem (see Appendix). The full utility of these questions will become clear after you have gone through the cases in Section Two.

HISTORY OF THE DOG

The first questions I usually ask are:

- Why did you pick that particular pet?
- Why did you pick that particular breed?
- Where was he obtained from?
- What was his temperament as a puppy?

These questions are extremely important for you to ask yourself. As I'll discuss more fully in Chapter Twelve on how to select puppies, the reasons for picking a dog and the

breed of dog can be vital in determining the kind of relationship you can have with your dog.

Recently I was called out to deal with a Great Pyrenees
named Bear who had become quite aggressive and had bitten
a neighbor. Bear's owners were an attractive couple in their
early thirties. Bob was a real estate planner and his wife,
Martha, worked at home making sweaters she sold to local
stores.

When I asked them what kind of dog they thought they
were getting when they got Bear, Bob replied, "A nice friendly
dog, a companion to Martha while I am away during the
day." Martha nodded in agreement.

Unfortunately, Bob and Martha were wrong about Pyrenees. Some Pyrenees are predisposed toward aggressive behavior as a result of careless breeding. Owners make this
mistake constantly—they select a dog without thinking
about what they really want. As time passes, owners who
want a passive dog discover that they have a very aggressive
one; or owners who want a playful dog realize they have a
very quiet one. This mismatch almost always leads to control problems with the dog.

As I questioned Bob and Martha I found out that Bear
had been separated from his mother during the first week!
The pet shop owner who sold Bear said that this had been
done so Bear could adjust quickly to people once adopted.
I told Bob and Martha that this was nonsense. The pet shop
owner encouraged separation in order to have another litter
of puppies to sell as soon as possible. The effect on Bear
was immeasurable, possibly a source of his extreme aggressiveness.

I'll discuss how owners *should* pick their puppy in
Chapter Twelve and how owners can test for a puppy's
temperament so that early signs of aggressiveness or pas-
sivity can be detected. You don't want to wind up like Bob
and Martha with a dog that requires a great deal of work.
But for now what is important for you to remember is that
you must carefully think about your dog's history. Many
clues to his behavioral problems will be found through this
process.

DOG PROBLEMS IN GENERAL

These questions are designed to move owners from vague descriptions of their dog problems to discuss, in very specific behavioral terms, what the problem is, how they have dealt with it in the past, exactly what the dog does, and when the problem occurs. What I'm trying to do is determine what the dog's real problem is and begin to decide on the best techniques for solving it.

The questions I ask include:

• How would you describe the problem?
• When did the problem begin?
• What steps have been taken to correct the problem?
• Is there a particular time of the day when the behavior is most likely to occur?
• What's the daily routine of your dog?
• Does this change on the weekend?

Asking owners to describe the problem may seem easy but it's not. I frequently hear very different versions of the problem when I talk to different members of a family. A young woman named Kristin recently called me in and said her terrier Ajax howled all the time. Kristin's elderly aunt, who lived with her, disagreed completely, saying, "Ajax only howls when the other dogs in the neighborhood start barking. Otherwise, he's a saint." So decide what the problem is.

Another inconsistency I hear from owners is, "Mr. McSoley, all of a sudden Bozo started howling day and night. I just can't figure out what got him going." Or, "One minute I was playing with him and the next he was snarling and trying to bite me." This is simply not true. Dog problems don't just happen. Knowing when the problem began gives you some idea of how long the behavior might continue, after you start a program of correction. The longer the problem has been going on, the more correction you'll have to do and for an extended period of time. If your dog has been frightened of thunderstorms for five years, for example, you aren't going to turn the problem around overnight with a few simple corrections. It's going to take consistent and faithful adherence to a conditioning program to make any headway.

After defining your problem and how long it has been going on, you should think about the steps you've taken to correct it. Have you hit the dog? Given him treats? Yelled and thrown chairs? Many owners have punished their dogs. Be honest, but don't feel guilty. What you did in the past is just information to be used to cure the problem.

After you have thought about your dog's problem inside the house, it's time to look carefully at the dog's behavior when he goes outside.

DOG'S BEHAVIOR OUTSIDE THE HOUSE

Some of the questions I ask are:

- Does he like to go for rides in the car?
- What is his behavior at gas stations, at toll booths?
- How is your pet's behavior in crowds?
- Does he run free in a yard, or is he fenced in?

How your dog behaves outside is crucial to understanding what is going on in an owner-pet relationship. Many owners have firm control of their dog inside the house, but lose it when they let the dog outside.

Owners often must take their dog for rides in the car. With some dogs this is no problem; with others, it is a major difficulty. Some dogs jump around in the car and bark continually. Others are quiet until they get near a toll booth or gas station. As soon as the attendant gets near the car they start barking. The dog is guarding his territory and taking the leader role when in the car, which will soon spell major trouble.

Owners need to note how their dog behaves when taken outside for exercise and how he acts when left outside by himself. If you are dragged along by the dog when out for a walk then the dog is in charge of the relationship. If you leave the dog outside for long periods of time, and the dog begins to rip up the yard, he's headed for destructive behavior inside the house. Having a long period of time when he is in charge of his environment leads your dog more and more to take the leader role.

DOG'S BEHAVIOR WITH OTHERS

- Does your dog like/tolerate/dislike strangers?
- Does he like/tolerate/dislike children?
- Does he like/tolerate/dislike your friends and relatives?
- Does he like/tolerate/dislike other dogs?

These questions help me understand what the dog's behavior is with others. A dog who's under control in the house with family members can suddenly become very aggressive with strangers, friends, children, or relatives. If he's brought outside for a walk and gets into frequent dogfights he may later begin to display aggressive behavior with humans.

Dogs who exhibit such aggressive behavior with people and dogs, will need extensive conditioning to enable owners to gain control.

DOG OBEDIENCE

- Has your dog been to obedience school?
- How did your dog do?
- Who went from your family?
- To whom is your pet most obedient?
- How do you correct him for misbehaviors?
- Are these corrections effective?

I ask these questions to find out what kind of obedience training a dog has had in the past and how owners have corrected their dogs. Unfortunately, the majority of owners I see have been to obedience schools and their dogs still won't obey. The problem isn't usually with the trainers. Rather, owners can't apply what they learn to their dog's behavior at home. Dogs who do well in training sessions will start to disobey at home if their owner can't build on what has been learned or if other family members work against maintaining discipline. It's important to take a hard look at whom the dog obeys in your family and why.

Owners have to examine how they are correcting their dog. We'll see many inappropriate corrections in the cases to come. There is only one rule regarding correction: IF IT ISN'T WORKING, STOP IT AND TRY SOMETHING ELSE.

HEALTH PROBLEMS AND DIETARY INFORMATION

I always ask some background questions about the dog's medical history and the kind of diet the dog is getting. It's important to have the dog periodically see the vet. He's the person best able to instruct you on a proper diet for your dog (housesoiling problems can result if you're overindulging the dog) and to examine Bozo for any medical situations that can be causing behavioral problems.

These are the major questions I ask every owner at our initial meeting. I then proceed to discuss what every owner must master—teaching the fundamentals of structure to his dog.

CHAPTER

3

Structure: The Five Basic Commands

W HEN I speak to owners about mastering the basic structures commands all I mean is: sit, stay, down, coming when called, and proper heeling. That's it, just five basic commands. They enable owners to control their dog and are the cornerstone of a happy and healthy relationship.

Unfortunately, most owners *cannot* get their dog to follow these commands—even if their pup has been to obedience school (at least 70 percent of my clients *have* been to obedience school). When I tell owners I want their dog to respond correctly to their commands one hundred percent of the time they look at me as if I were a madman. But there's no other standard. If you carefully follow what I tell you, you'll achieve complete obedience from your dog.

In all of these exercises I want you to think about what you want the dog to learn, what you're teaching him, and lastly, the best way to teach him.

I break the basics into three phases: initial teaching; simple reinforcement; and finally, advanced reinforcement. In this chapter I talk about the basic structures. In the next two chapters I show you how to use a choke collar and then an electric collar to speed up your dog's response to the basics.

Don't be intimidated. Follow along and you'll see how you can do these exercises quickly and well.

SIT

You probably think that when you give your dog the command "Sit" he understands the "idea" of the sit position. That's simply not so. Think for a second what a dog does when his owner tells him to sit. He *moves* from the standing position *to* the sitting position. Sit to a dog is the *act* of moving from the standing position to the sitting position. This is what the exercise means.

Now how did I show my dog, Jake (whom you met on the cover of this book), when he was an eight-week-old puppy how to sit on command? First, without Jake seeing me, I took five or six pieces of his dry dog food in my hand. I then knelt in front of him with a piece of his dog food between my right thumb and forefinger. I held the food *close* to his nose—about an inch away—told him "Sit" and then brought my hand slightly above and a little behind his head. Jake brought his head up and back to follow the food. When his head went back, it forced his rear into a neat little sit. I immediately said "Good sit" and put the food into his mouth. That was Jake's first sit.

That's all you have to do with your dog. If your dog jumps for the food, as many dogs do the first few times they're being taught, simply bring the food *down* in front of him and begin again. *Don't yell at him.* Dogs hear almost five times better than people, so always use a normal voice tone. Yelling accomplishes nothing, except to break the dog's concentration and make it more difficult for him to respond to your command. Remember, at this point your dog has no idea what you're doing, much less what "Sit" means.

The proper hand motion for sit.

So how does your dog eventually put it together? Repetition. It's the same principle that underlies advertising. Repeat a jingle or phrase enough and consumers internalize it. The same holds for dogs. Just keep repeating the exercise.

On the first day you should do the sit exercise six times in a row or three times twice a day. You should be kneeling directly in front of the dog when you do this exercise. The next day you should repeat this sequence but standing. When you say "Sit" you should bring up your hand that holds the food up, moving it about three to four inches above your waist. This helps reinforce the dog's upward head movement and focuses his attention on you.

This exercise sequence, simple as it is, must be repeated twice daily, once in the morning and once at night, until the dog is sitting *consistently*, which should take a few days. That is, when you tell him "Sit" and bring your hand holding the food in front of him and he sits *every time*, he's put it together.

All dogs may not adapt this quickly. It may take several weeks. But that's up to the pup. Just keep on doing it.

Some minor points. The food treat should be very small, no bigger than dime size. Make certain your dog is sitting when he gets the treat, the "Good sit," and a pat. He can get up after the pat. If he sits and gets up quickly, and you give him food when he's back on his feet, you've rewarded him for standing, not sitting.

After you've gotten consistent sits from your dog you should begin slipping him food every other time he sits. Why? Because *intermittent reinforcement is stronger than consecutive reinforcement!* Although that may seem strange to you, behavioral scientists know that intermittent reinforcement increases the desire for the dog to work for his reward. He is inclined to respond faster and *not get bored*. So, don't give him food every time. But always a quick "Good sit." After about a month you can phase out the food completely, but take your time.

If you're teaching sit to an older dog, you may have to put a bit of pressure on his hindquarters when you start. Simply push down with your free hand and apply just enough easy, consistent pressure to start him. But only do this until he begins sitting. He doesn't need any extra assistance after that.

All family members should do this exercise as well as all the basic commands with the dog. Everyone in the house has to be a leader or your dog will try to become second-in-command behind the person teaching the basics.

STAY

This is the simplest of all basic structures because your dog doesn't do anything except not move. Here's how to teach your dog to stay in two weeks.

Stand in front of Bozo, facing him. Have in the crevice between your thumb and palm a food treat. Give him the "Sit" command. Right after the dog sits, bring your hands, palms facing your dog, so they bracket your face, about five or six inches away. Stare right at your pup and say "Stay." You should be standing approximately two and one half to three feet directly in front of him.

Remain in front of Bozo for about three to four seconds, then take a step forward, moving right beside him, tell him "Good dog" and give him a food treat. Repeat this exercise three more times on the first day. That's all there is to it. Continue to do this for two weeks along with sit.

Now if Bozo doesn't stay that's okay. Don't correct him for not doing it right. Bozo has absolutely no idea what's expected of him. But don't reward him with a food treat. All you should do is to bring the dog back to the same spot, tell him "Sit" and repeat the stay command.

Jake, had particular trouble with this exercise when he was a pup. He broke the first six times I tried "Stay." On the seventh time he stayed, not because he understood what I wanted, but because he was so confused that he did nothing. Then I gave him a reward. After a few sitting-because-of-confusion responses, the light bulb went on in Jake's head.

Remember, praise your dog verbally every time you return to him. Don't praise as you walk toward the dog; start when you're back beside him. There's a sound reason for this approach. I don't want Bozo to anticipate your praise by breaking his stay and coming out to meet you halfway. I also don't want you calling your dog to you to end the stay. This may teach him to be unsteady in the stay position, since he anticipates being called to you and then getting praised.

Your dog should always be praised for staying, not for breaking the stay and returning to you. This is why dogs

The proper position to teach stay . . .

become confused in the stay exercise and why they will not consistently hold a stay. Only when your dog is completely reliable in staying should you begin calling him out of it.

Remember also that from the very beginning you should condition your dog to a release word from "Stay." I use the word "Okay." When I tell my dog Jake to "Stay," he stays until I give the release word "Okay" or I call him to me. Jake never heard a correction from me on "Stay" until I was absolutely certain he fully understood what it meant. At that point, I would simply say in a stern voice, "Hey, dummy, you know better than that" as I brought him back to the point from where he broke. Then I would simply repeat the exercise. When he did it correctly, I praised him.

Owners make one major mistake with this exercise— they attempt building too much distance from their dog too

. . . and move beside Bozo and say "Good dog."

early in the learning process. I tell my clients they should first increase time, then distance. Once your dog is staying consistently, you should begin to move straight back a couple of steps at a time. Don't go over ten feet. After you have built up distance straight back, you should add variety to the exercise. Instead of dropping straight back, move a few degrees to the right or left. Start creating an imaginary circle as you move around your dog.

Also, after your dog is clearly aware of what "Stay" means, it is not necessary for you to keep holding your hands in front of you. Your hands are initially helpful in focusing the dog's attention.

As with the sit exercise, you should begin intermittent food reinforcement after your dog starts to stay with regularity.

My last point concerns eye contact. The stay exercise is one place where you'll certainly need it. For example, when you're working on stay outside and Bozo is watching a squirrel scampering up a tree, guess where his attention is focused. You can focus his attention on you through an excellent exercise that I picked up from Jim Dobbs, a professional trainer in Marysville, California. With a young puppy it's simple to teach. Hold a food treat at arm's length out to your side and then say, "Good dog." And then give the pup the treat. Pup is sitting in front of you looking at the food treat at arm's length. As you say "Look," bring your hand toward your face. Do this four or five times at each session until when you say "Look" the puppy immediately looks directly at you. You quickly add "Good dog." This exercise is effective with older dogs as well.

Now three weeks have passed since you started following my program and your dog has learned how to sit and stay. Let's teach him how to lie down.

DOWN

First of all, you have to decide what it is that you want "Down" to mean. Is it lie down? Or is it part of catchall phrases such as "Get down off the furniture," "Get down off of Aunt Sue," and so on. If you use it this way, then I suggest you use another word for lie down. I don't care what that word is—"drop" or "flop" might be appropriate.

You might elect to use "charge," commonly used in England. I once had a client who had a one-hundred-pound German shepherd. This gentleman took great delight in commanding "Charge" to his dog to the terror of anyone standing near him.

"Down" should mean to lie down—Rover assuming a prone position, on his stomach, front legs extended.

Here's how I taught Jake this position. I got down on one knee and I told Jake to come over to me. I said "Sit" and when he did, I took my right hand—holding food treat approximately four inches away from his nose and parallel

Bozo follows my hand . . .

. . .to a proper down.

with the ground—said "Down" and then dropped my hand *straight* down to the ground and then moved it slightly forward on the ground. Jake followed my hand down and did it on his first try! I popped a food treat into his mouth and told him "Good down." I then repeated this exercise three more times in a row the first day. Eventually you can stand when practicing this exercise.

If your dog is reluctant to lie down that easily I've a couple of suggestions. First, do the exercise several times in a row, perhaps as many as ten repetitions, before making any changes. If at the end of these sessions you're still having problems, do this exercise: Come up to Rover's right-hand side and with your left hand take his left leg, and with your right hand grab his right leg. Then simply slide his legs out from under him!

Some dogs are reluctant to lie down immediately because it's a frightening experience for them. You can reduce this fear in your dog through patience, persistence, and firmness. Remember, when the dog lies down, give him food and praise. Soon you'll find that merely telling him "Down" and bringing your right hand down does the trick.

COMING WHEN CALLED

The number-one training problem I deal with is not coming when called. There are several ways Fido doesn't come: he may ignore his owner, he may respond by coming halfway and beginning a little game of tag, or he may kick in the afterburners and roar off to the next county.

I try to get clients to examine the reasons their dog won't come. Are the circumstances under which he is called usually unpleasant? For example, do you call your dog just before you're going to work and you're intending on shutting him in the house for the day? Fido's not stupid; he doesn't want to do that. Or have you hit your dog the last time he didn't come quickly enough to please you? Well, your furry friend isn't coming back for another beating if he can help it.

Some dogs won't come when called if owners wait too long to teach the command. With Jake I began clapping my hands and playing the coming-when-called game when he was nine weeks old. Later, when I first brought him outside, I'd walk away from him, get a little distance, clap my hands, blow my whistle and give him a wealth of praise when he caught up with me. Coming when called started out as fun for both of us. Incidentally, my praise was accompanied by a dime-sized piece of American cheese. This was the only command for which I used cheese as a food reward. I wanted it to be special for Jake. Coming when called has to be enjoyable and exciting for the dog. If it isn't, somewhere down the road you are probably going to have a problem.

Now let's talk about getting your dog to come. To begin with, your dog has an option—he can come, or not. You cannot *demand* that he come to you. If you do, you're simply setting up a battle of wills, which isn't the basis of a good relationship.

Here's what I want you to do. Go to your local sporting goods store and pick up a *small* plastic referee's whistle. You don't need anything more expensive than that. I like a whistle for several reasons. Because of its pitch, it's more exciting than your voice. A whistle also gives a consistent call. When owners are angry, tired, or frustrated they use different inflections in their calling, thereby creating inconsistency in the command. Finally, a whistle can be used by all members of the family, so your dog is always called in the same manner, regardless of voice quality or tone.

Where you practice this command is very important. I don't want you to start in your front yard. This is usually the worst place to begin since you've probably lost a few coming-when-called battles here already. Start in your house. This may seem crazy, because Bozo usually comes when called when he is inside. But I've a good reason for this— when you teach this outside you have a much greater problem controlling the dog.

Several years ago I had a client who had a three-year-old borzoi, a Russian wolfhound named Ivan. Ivan's owner, a Dr. Rose, asked me if I would whistle-train his dog to come. I said I'd be happy to oblige. There was a local school not far from Dr. Rose's house that had a very large fenced track. Dr. Rose suggested we use that area for training purposes. Having never seen one of these dogs run flat out, I agreed.

When we got to the track, the good doctor let Ivan off his leash and he immediately began to race around the track, lapping a group of high school runners as if they were standing still. Thoroughly impressed with Ivan's speed, I said to the doctor, "He sure can move, Doc." A sly smile spread across his face and he said, "Oh, he's not running yet, just warming up his legs." Suddenly, Ivan seemed to explode away from the track and in a flash of dust reappeared some two hundred yards from the spot where I last saw him.

"Mr. McSoley," Dr. Rose said, "shall I toot the whistle now."

I gazed at the borzoi in the distance and said, "Doc, you can blow the pea out of the damn whistle, but he's never going to come when called."

Even if your dog doesn't move at Ivan's speed, training him outside is asking for trouble; there are just too many distractions.

Here's how you should start. Tonight, when your dog is lying peacefully next to you, take the referee's whistle I told you to buy and blow it three times, which should get his attention. Immediately give the pup some cheese and a lot of praise. Do this two more times, then call it quits for the evening. All you want your dog to do is open his mouth. Don't expect him to move.

Repeat this procedure twice the next day, three times at each session. In each session give him a piece of cheese and take five minutes to do the exercise.

Do this one more day. Then you're ready for the next phase—distance. At some point during the evening on the fourth day, move a little bit away from your faithful companion and hit the whistle. When Rover comes to you, give him a food treat and a ton of praise. Do this twice each day. Gradually increase the distance. Sometimes you should play hide and seek with him. Rover should work at finding you. When he does, make it exciting for him by praising him loudly and clapping your hands energetically.

Do this for two weeks before you attempt taking him outside without a leash.

When you bring Rover outside, go to a place he's never been. This increases his dependence on you and improves your chances of making him come when called.

Take him for a walk in a field, and when he gets in front of you, approximately forty to fifty feet, turn, and begin walking away from him. Then start blowing that whistle and put some energy into it! This makes the exercise exciting. When Rover turns around and sees you're walking away from him he should start scampering after you. When he gets to you, immediately give him a cheese treat and lots of praise. Do this two or three times more within thirty minutes and end the session. Don't expect perfection at this point, just look for some positive response.

The more walks like this the better. Don't let him loose on your property until you have had at least two dozen sessions in the field.

Now as an alternative to this approach, some experts recommend hooking the dog to a line and reeling him in like Charley the Tuna. This works for a few dogs, but for the majority of dogs I've worked with, it's still forcing him to come back. I want you to get Bozo to come because he wants to. So I prefer the praise and cheese approach.

But please, *never* punish a dog learning to come for not coming fast enough. Remember, coming when called means two things—get over here and do it now. We tend to take both things for granted. Your beloved pet might understand only get over here and be a little fuzzy on when. So if he stops to smell the roses on the way over, don't give him a rap on the head for tardiness.

HEELING

Showing someone how to heel your dog is like learning how to play tennis or do karate from a book. It's relatively easy to tell how to do it and practically impossible for the reader to master. However, I've seen some ideas on the subject that are quite different from those held by most trainers and I'd like to share them with you.

I begin with this principle: the dog has the option of either heeling or not. The only time he doesn't have the option is when you're holding the lead (leash) tight and then that's not heeling. You see, most owners don't take their dog for a walk—their dog takes them for a drag. Everyone is familiar with this sight: Nanooke of the North out front, owner in tow. It resembles a cut-down version of the Iditarod—the Alaskan dog race—except the owner plays the role of the sled.

It doesn't have to be this way. The first step is to change your thinking. Your dog has an option to heel or not, whether he's on the lead or off. Doing it the other way—constantly holding your dog next to you using the strangulation method—is merely restraint, not control. And it sure as hell isn't very pleasant.

I also disagree with the age-old method of walking around telling Fido "Heel" and then jerking him back into line time after time after time.

The way I want you to begin is to put some mental pressure on your dog, not on you. I taught my dog, Jake, to heel by mentally pressuring him. I begin by having him on my left side, sitting, with the lead slack. I simply told him, "Jake, heel," and stepped off at a normal pace, leading off with my left foot. Of course, Jake took off like gangbusters, getting to the end of the lead in no time. But just as he was about to come up short, I commanded "Heel" and immediately gave the lead a very quick, firm snap. Jake gave a yelp, and turned around toward me, only to see that I had already turned 180 degrees and was beginning to walk off in the opposite direction.

The second Jake saw me, I slapped my left leg with my left hand and cheerfully called "Good dog, good dog." Jake ran after me—and past me, only to have the same thing happen again: "Heel," followed immediately by the quick, firm snap, and my changing direction to the right 180 degrees, followed by praise.

I had already turned 180 degrees and was beginning to walk off in the opposite direction.

It didn't take Jake long to figure out that whenever he went out in front of me, he never knew what direction I was going to take and that he would always hear the command "Heel." Also, the only time the lead was ever taut is when I snapped it. It was slack at all other times. So Jake, smart dog that he is, decided rather quickly that as long as he walked by my side and focused on me, he kept the lead slack and got praise. After Jake got better at right turns, I then began making left turns as well. (On left turns you say, "Heel" and snap straight back.)

Because the snap on the lead was always preceded by the command "Heel," Jake began to understand that when he heard "Heel" and he came back to my left side very fast, then he wouldn't feel the snap on his neck. Study the photos on the next page; they should help you put this in perspective.

Your dog should understand what "Heel" means after *one* session. Most owners are amazed when I tell them this. But if you are correctly executing the snaps and turns, your dog will learn quickly. After that, it's only a matter of repetition.

When should a dog heel? Whenever he walks with you, unless you give him a release command such as "Okay." Is this overly rigid? No, because you're the leader and Bozo will be very content walking next to you. I can bring Jake into downtown Boston without being embarrassed at his jumping up on someone, or accidentally tripping people walking past. I even bring him into stores at times in order to reinforce his manners, even though most managers frown on having dogs in their stores. I have found many managers to be tolerant of me and Jake, as long as I have Jake under control.

My favorite story about teaching heeling involves a German shepherd named Max and his owner Sara. This young lawyer called me because she could no longer heel Max—he was always out in front when they walked, zealously protecting her. When anyone approached within thirty feet of Sara, Max would bark, snarl, and then begin lunging at the person.

I told Sara I would help her teach Max how to heel in

Pull Bozo back with a hand, say "heel" and snap the leash . . .

. . . and walk in the opposite direction, saying "Goodbye."

one session. Sara was a bit skeptical. "Mr. McSoley," she said, "you haven't seen this dog in action. He's very frightening." I just nodded, and said I wanted to give it a try. I walked over to Max and commanded him to sit, which he did very slowly, staring at me constantly. After a second sit, I told him, "Max, heel," and I stepped off smartly. So did Max, covering his six feet of lead in short order. Just as he was about to get to the end, I turned around, commanding "Heel" and snapping the lead sharply.

Max let out a throaty growl. His eyes opened wide, he showed his teeth and then he tore after me. I've been charged before so I quickly sidestepped him, catching him up short with the lead. Then I yanked him right off the ground, holding that eighty-five-pound package of fury in the air for a few seconds until he became calm. I slowly released him, and told him to sit. Max obeyed, looking at me completely bewildered.

Over the next forty-five minutes I worked Max on heeling, getting him better and better, until he was walking next to me with the lead completely slack, turning when I turned, stopping when I stopped, sitting nicely when I gave the command to sit.

Then Sara, Max, and I took a walk up a main Boston thoroughfare, coming close to a hundred people, who passed within less than a foot of us. Max never even made a sideways glance toward these people. I made Sara heel him as well. Max did as well with her as he did with me.

What transformation had taken place? Why was I so certain that Max wouldn't bite some poor guy on the street? Max simply learned that he was not in charge. He was no longer responsible *for* Sara, but responsible *to* Sara. His job was to follow, not to lead. This is the lesson all heeling teaches.

CHAPTER
4

Simple Reinforcement: Avoidance Collar

IN this chapter and the next I'll show you how to increase your control over your dog by using what are called choke collars and electric collars.

The basic structures I've taught are called positive reinforcers. All this means is that when you tell your dog to sit, he responds and you reinforce him by rewarding him either through praise or food. Positive reinforcement is an excellent initial method of conditioning your dog.

It is now time to begin what I call simple reinforcement. A more scientific definition for this is negative reinforcement. There are two basic types of simple reinforcement— escape training and avoidance training. Escape training simply means that a particular response terminates an unpleasant feeling. An example of this is when a dog runs into his doghouse to escape the rain that's getting him wet.

Or let's say you've stopped at a red light. The light turns green, and immediately the driver behind you starts yelling at you before you begin to move. At the next light you watch the light more carefully; this time when the light turns green you react quicker, trying to *escape* the wrath of the driver screaming a blue streak at you. In a behavioral scientist's terms this little situation looks like this:

Cue	Aversive	Response
Green light	Abusive Driver	You drive away

Avoidance training is merely an extension or progression of escape training. Let's go back to our harassed driver. We're hovering over him in a helicopter and our Looney Tunes driver is still behind him. We follow them for six blocks and we notice something interesting happening. As soon as the light turns green, the first driver hits the gas pedal so quickly that the guy behind doesn't have time to holler. Our friend has learned to *avoid* the abuse—by performing the behavior quicker.

So that's what we're going to teach the pup. How to do what you want him to do reliably and quickly. Remember our dog escaping the rain by running into the doghouse. What happens to him after repeated thunderstorms? As soon

The electric collar and transmitter.

as he hears the thunder, he runs into his doghouse. He's learned to avoid the rain altogether.

Here's how this looks in behavioral terms:

ESCAPE TRAINING

Cue	Aversive	Response
Thunder	Rain	Runs into house

AVOIDANCE TRAINING

Cue	followed by	Response
Thunder		Runs into house

Escape training and avoidance training are the conditioning principles that underlie the use of choke collars and electric collars respectively. When the collars are used correctly, a dog learns he controls his destiny by acting in a positive way to avoid pain. This builds his confidence and helps him be a more willing partner to you.

By using a choke collar you can teach simple reinforcement to your dog the same way I taught Jake, or rather how Jake taught himself. "Choke" is an unfortunate modifier since this collar should never be used to choke or cause real pain to a dog. That's why I call them avoidance collars—the principles of escape/avoidance are what makes them work effectively.

But first a word about the kind of collar you should use. It should meet two important criteria. First, it must fit properly, and second, it should be made of sturdy metal links. Both Lambert Kay and Deva are good brand names. I prefer flat links, close together, as I feel they slide more smoothly and release more quickly than the open type link.

Fit, though, is either correct or incorrect. There should be approximately two and one half inches of slack after the collar is on the dog's neck. You should place the collar on your dog this way: Take the collar and hold it in a vertical line. Feeding the chain through the bottom ring so as to create a closed circle with the rings interconnected. Put your left thumb in the top loop and your right hand on the other end of the loop to form the letter P. When you've done this, you're ready to slip the collar over your dog's head.

Now I want to show you how to use your avoidance collar correctly. You can do this either indoors or outdoors.

Decide which side you are going to work the dog. You *don't* have to work the pup on your left side if you prefer the right. It makes no difference to Bozo. Most experts and books recommend the left because the majority of people are right handed and therefore find it easier to have their dog on their "off" side. As a rule, bird hunters work their dogs on their "off gun" side, the left, for obvious safety factors. They prefer shooting the bird to shooting their dog.

Once you have the collar and lead on, and have decided which side to work, here's how you reinforce the first basic structure—sit. Practice this technique inside your house; any room with a fair amount of space will do.

With your dog standing by your side hold the lead fairly short, but with some slack. There should be *no* pressure on the dog's neck. Then you tell your dog "Sit" and immediately (no more than half a second) bring the leash straight up, putting some pressure on the collar and therefore the dog's neck. Hold the pressure until your dog is completely in the sit position.

The split second your pup sits, release the pressure and say "Good dog." You don't have to cause him pain. Don't pull his front paws off the ground or jerk him around, just sustain enough pressure for him to be uncomfortable. Timing is the key. This exercise helps Rover learn that when he hears "Sit" and he sits, he escapes the pressure on his neck. That's why your timing is so important. Behavioral scientists tell us that longer than half a second is too long a time to elapse because the dog might become confused as to why the pressure is being applied. He must make the association in order to learn. So don't be slow on the draw.

No matter how long it takes Bozo to sit, hold the pressure. Ten seconds, two minutes. Just keep holding the pressure. Eventually he'll sit. When he does, release the pressure. From the dog's point of view *you're not relieving the pressure—he's relieving the pressure.* You must understand this point. When the dog releases the pressure, he begins to realize that sitting *feels good*. He thinks, "I feel good when I sit." That's what you want the dog to understand.

While you're holding pressure on the lead don't repeat the command "Sit." Take a patience pill (you'll be learning to take a few of these before you properly condition your dog) and keep your cool.

This exercise, of course, should be done only after you've taught your dog how to sit. Its purpose is to help your dog obey this basic command faster and more consistently. You should do this exercise for five minutes, at least twice daily. Your dog will sit more and more quickly. That's what you want—simple consistency. You should be having fun doing this, because you are gaining firmer control over Fido; your dog should be having fun because he is gaining confidence in himself and his ability to please you. Eventually, he'll sit quite quickly.

Once you've become comfortable with this command, you should put some pressure on Bozo to pay attention to you. With him on the lead, let him wander two or three feet from you. When he faces away from you, say "Sit" and immediately follow with pressure on the collar. He should sit when he hears the command. When Bozo becomes consistent in his response, walk him around the room, periodically telling him to sit. Use the lead and keep walking. Your dog should stop and sit when told even though you continue to walk. When that response becomes almost automatic, go out and pour yourself a drink—you've earned it. And give your dog an extra scratch behind his ears—he's earned it. You're finally becoming a team.

REINFORCING STAY

By this time it should be clearer why I like "avoidance" rather than "choke" collar. Your dog learns to sit so quickly now that he beats you to the punch; you can no longer begin to put pressure on the collar because "Sit" and his response are now so close. He knows if he obeys quickly enough he avoids pressure.

Now I want you to forget the word "Stay." Not the command, just the word. From this point on, "Sit" should mean to sit and to stay, until the dog gets the next directive from you. What I taught you initially changes a little now, but it should not be hard for you to adjust. All you need is a little time and some consistency.

Tell your dog "Sit." When he sits, simply say "Good dog" quietly. Don't say another word, just stand there and wait. Eventually your dog will break the sit. He'll either stand or lie down. That's no good. The minute he breaks, repeat "Sit" and apply the pressure. If he breaks again, repeat again. Repeat until Fido stays in the sit position for a few seconds. Quietly tell him "Good dog," and at the end of the time period tell him "Okay," walk away a couple of feet, and pull the lead toward you to get him to release.

If he won't move, repeat "Okay" and clap your hands, so that he will break the sit/stay. From this moment on, he should never leave sit/stay on his own. He should always wait until commanded otherwise. Little by little increase both the time and distance for the sit/stay. It won't be long before Bozo is holding sit very well. At this point, he knows that while "Sit" means to drop his hindquarters, it also means to remain in the sit position until you tell him what you want him to do next.

REINFORCING DOWN

Here's how I want you to do this exercise. Have your dog sit. Facing the dog, hold the lead slack in your left hand (if you're on your dog's right side), and give the down signal with your right hand. Tell your dog "Down" and before he begins to lie down, bend over and quickly *pull straight down* with the collar, putting just enough pressure on him so his head is hanging down (don't angle the lead to any side or the dog won't go down correctly). Then just hold everything in that position. Let him make the next move.

When he lies down, praise him. You don't have to release pressure on the collar—he's done it himself by lying down. If he sits there, just hold. Rover may begin to flop around like a fish out of water. Just hold. Eventually, your dog will lie down. It's the only way he can shut off the pressure from the collar.

Repeat this exercise several more times. Two short, daily sessions should do the trick. Pretty soon when you give the down command, your dog will drop consistently and quickly.

After this has happened, give the down command from the standing position, using the same routine if he balks. You may put your foot on the lead rather than your hand so you no longer have to lean over.

I demonstrated this method to a client recently who owned an eighteen-month-old male rottweiler named Boston who not only wouldn't lie down, but would snarl and try to bite his owner when given the command. It took two weeks for the owner to get Boston to lie down using my method but it did the trick and he didn't get bitten either. The secret was faith in the method, patience, calmness, and firmness.

Incidentally, you should be doing these commands in all rooms in the house, as well as outside, where there are considerably more distractions.

REINFORCING COMING WHEN CALLED

When doing this exercise it is often useful to attach a twenty-five-foot line (check cord) to your dog. It is best to take Bozo to an open field (or a park if you live in an urban area) where the line can run smoothly.

When you begin this exercise, your dog should be facing away from you and the pressure on the lead should remain *until* he comes toward you; then you turn off the pressure. In the field, let your dog go out to just about the end of the line, hit your whistle and immediately follow this with a quick jerk. When the dog comes in, then give him praise. He should sit right in front of you.

Use as little cord pressure as possible. Don't make your

dog cord-conditioned—that is, that he responds only when he's on the cord.

The avoidance collar exercises should be used to reinforce the basic commands after your dog has sufficiently mastered them. The collar's purpose is to get the dog to react quickly and should be used every day until this response is achieved. After that you can stop. But if you're having trouble with any or all commands resume the collar. As I like to say to my clients, your dog is like a hinge on a door. If you don't maintain the hinge through proper oiling the door will move slower and slower. So don't neglect Bozo. Use the collar for both your sakes.

Advanced Reinforcement: Electric Collar

A S soon as I mention electric dog collars to most of my clients they think it's a form of torture. That's completely wrong. An electric collar is a humane, safe, and effective *tool* to help you and your dog achieve a better relationship. If your dog is doing his basic commands well, then you don't need this kind of help. But I recommend the electric collar if you're still having trouble with the pup even though you used the avoidance collar properly, or if you just want to achieve more with the dog in terms of the basic commands.

I want to separate fact from fiction regarding electric collars.

Fiction The electric collar must cause pain to be effective.

Fact An unpleasant feeling (aversive) is necessary; real pain is not. In fact, real pain can reduce the effectiveness of the electric collar.

Fiction The electric collar's only purpose is to punish incorrect behavior.

Fact   The electric collar's most important benefit is its unique ability to assist you in *reinforcing* good behavior.

Fiction Electric collars are easy to use.

Fact   Unless you are thoroughly familiar with the proper method of conditioning, and have experience using the collar, you should seek assistance from a professional *qualified* in its proper use.

Fiction Electric collars can be used on dogs of any age and any weight.

Fact   The collar should only be used on a dog who is over a year old and over twenty pounds.

Recently, I worked with a four-year-old pointer named Patrick who was a marvelous companion to his owners, Joan and Mark. Patrick had one major problem—when he'd go with his owners to a nearby high school field for exercise in the morning, he'd take off for the woods that bordered the field on both sides. Although Joan and Mark had taught Patrick coming when called, the lure of the woods was far more powerful. They tried tempting Patrick back with food, using a "check cord," and the old standby, screaming and chasing after him. Nothing worked.

Mark and Joan became increasingly worried that Patrick could get harmed and decided to curtail his running loose. Now a new problem arose—because Patrick couldn't release his energy, he became restless in the house, pacing, getting into closets, and so forth.

When I looked at Patrick I realized he was a well-trained dog but wasn't as responsive as he should be in coming when called and heeling. Heeling I could straighten out in a short time but I suggested the electric collar as the way to deal with the coming-when-called problem. When I suggested the collar Joan looked as if the Marquis de Sade was standing in her kitchen. But as I explained how the collar would help extend control over distance, Joan relaxed.

After a month of working with the collar, Patrick was

coming when called like a champion. Patrick and Joan were very happy with the results and could now trust their dog off the leash. They and Patrick had a sense of freedom they'd never known before.

How did the collar work? The one I'll be discussing is manufactured by Tri-Tronics, Inc., located in Tucson, Arizona. It's the one I use, and I've found it to be excellent. These collars come in a range of prices, with even the most advanced unit priced well under a thousand dollars.

All Tri-Tronics collars consist of the following:

- Hand-held radio-controlled transmitter
- An active dog collar (receiver)
- A dummy (inactive) collar
- A test light that tells the user the unit is properly charged
- Five different plugs, numbered one to five, providing five different levels of electrical stimulation.

Used properly, these collars help you achieve everything you can accomplish using the avoidance collar (and more), except by remote control. Coming when called, for example, can be reinforced from anywhere. In fact, all the basic structures can be reinforced. Remember in the last section how you learned to use the avoidance collar properly. It involved escape training and avoidance training. With the avoidance collar you're applying mechanical pressure; with the electric collar you're using electrical pressure.

The particular unit I've been using is a Model A1-90LR. It's sophisticated, but easy to master. There are three buttons located on the hand-held transmitter. When the yellow button is pressed, your dog will hear a quick beep. Let's call this a warning beep. When the red button is pressed, your dog will hear this same beep, immediately followed by electrical stimulation (shock). As long as the button is pressed the dog continues to feel the pressure (shock), up to a maximum of ten seconds, at which point a circuit breaker automatically terminates the shock. There is also a third button on this particular unit. When this green button is pressed, the dog hears a monotone hum. This is pressed when the dog completes the correct behavior—sort of an electrical "Good dog."

I introduced Jake to the collar using the green button. While I was still using the avoidance collar, I also had Jake wearing the electric collar. I'd tell him "Sit" while we were taking a walk, and as he completed the sit I'd press the green button, at the same time telling him "Good dog." Within a short time, when he sat I'd merely press the green button, not necessarily telling him "Good dog," and Jake would wag his tail when he heard that hum. It was relaxing to him.

In the last chapter, you'll recall, when I spoke of simple reinforcement using the avoidance collar I didn't use the collar to correct incorrect behavior. The same is true of the electric collar. Now let's say you want to reinforce the sit command using the electric collar. Here's how it's done.

REINFORCING SIT

Since I don't want you using the electric collar without the assistance of a qualified professional (not just a dog trainer, but a professional in the use of the collar), I'm only going to explain how it is used with one command—"Sit." You have the leash, the avoidance collar, and the electric collar on Bozo. You tell Bozo "Sit," at the same time pressing the red button on the electric collar; immediately after, pull straight up with the avoidance collar. Bozo hears the quick warning beep, followed immediately by both mechanical pressure (avoidance collar) as well as electrical pressure (electric collar). Continue both pressures as Bozo goes through the process of sitting. The second Bozo sits, you immediately take your thumb off the red button, as well as slackening the leash. Follow this by pressing the green button while at the same time saying "Good dog."

After several repetitions of this Bozo understands that sitting turns off both mechanical pressure and electrical pressure. Your dog is effectively escaping the stimulation by simply doing what you tell him—the first time you tell him. Here's what's going on:

cue - - -warning beep - - -aversive - - -response - - -reinforcer

"Sit"   Beep   Shock   Bozo sits   Green button

This is merely advanced escape training. As Bozo begins to understand that sitting turns off both types of pressure, then the avoidance collar is no longer necessary. Instead, the electric collar provides all the aversive necessary. Bozo begins to sit faster in order to escape the shock. Before long, when you tell him "Sit," he sits immediately. At this point, you progress to the yellow button. It works like this:

cue- - - - - - -warning beep- - - - - - -response- - - - - - -reinforcer

"Sit"   Beep   Dog sits   Green button

When you've reached this point, your dog has realized that he can avoid the shock altogether by sitting immediately. Eventually he'll learn that sitting both quickly and consistently cancels the necessity for the warning beep.

Here's the next situation:

cue - - - - - - - - - - - - - -response - - - - - - - - - - - - - -reinforcer

"Sit"   Dog sits   Green button

Now think back to my example of the dog running into his doghouse to escape the rain. The electric collar accomplishes the same type of conditioning. At this point if your dog is thirty feet in front of you, and you command "Sit," Bozo will sit. Why? Because he's learned how to succeed. You've helped to produce a far more self-confident dog. He now understands that by doing the correct thing (sit) he can completely avoid the aversive altogether. He's now master of his own destiny. He thinks that he has beaten the system, except that he has beaten the system your way!

Remember, you're not punishing Bozo for not sitting.

In punishment, the aversive ("No!," shaking by the scruff of the neck, and other similar actions) follows the behavior.

PUNISHMENT

(Mis) Behavior	**Aversive**
Bozo jumps on the counter	"No!"

With the electric collar (and the avoidance collar), the proper behavior is *preceded* by the aversive:

ELECTRIC COLLAR

Cue	**Aversive**	**Behavior**
"Sit"	Shock	Dog sits

The man chiefly responsible for the development of the A1-90LR collar is Daniel Tortora, Ph.D., dog trainer, animal behavioral therapist and author.

A word of caution. If you're prone to train out of anger, forget the collar. If you're interested in purchasing the collar merely as a "last resort," you are approaching it from the wrong standpoint. Nor should it ever be purchased out of retribution. If you are thinking about using the collar to correct behavioral problems, it can be effective in certain problem areas. However, using the electric collar to correct inappropriate behavior should never be attempted by a novice.

We've now completed the basics of structuring your dog, including both simple and advanced reinforcement. Let's see how my rules and concepts work.

SECTION

II

CHAPTER
6

Aggressive Behavior

B ILL Johnson greeted me at the door with a rebuke. "It's about time you got here McSoley, you're damn inconvenient."

I've a tendency to be late for appointments, since I hate leaving a client until I've accomplished my goals for that session. But Johnson's testiness was uncalled for—I was only twenty minutes behind schedule.

"Don't just stand there, come on in, damn it. We've got a lot to talk about."

I could tell immediately that Johnson was used to getting his way. A small man in his mid-forties, he was nattily dressed—tweed jacket, brown slacks, and an ascot tucked neatly inside a powder-blue shirt—and his hair was stylishly slicked back, 1930's-style. He looked every inch the imperious executive at leisure and I, undoubtedly in his mind, was a hired underling who was tardy.

Johnson led me through the foyer of his elegant Tudor house into his study, where I was greeted by a scene of absolute chaos. Fur coats, books, bedsheets, sports jackets, empty TV dinner trays, shirts, lamps were tossed everywhere. Boxes were piled upon boxes and a heavy layer of dust covered the room. I felt as if I'd stepped into a second-hand antique store.

"It's a real shithole, isn't it?" Johnson said. "Been this way since my divorce. I'm always traveling for business so I never have time to sort things out."

He looked directly at me and said, "What the hell are you going to do about Mandrake? He's scaring the crap out of me. He growls and shows his teeth, barking like a sub-machine gun."

I thought it ironic that Johnson might be a powerhouse businessman during the day, but Mandrake had him un-hinged. I asked him to tell me about Mandrake.

Because of his traveling, Johnson spent little time with Mandrake. His wife didn't have much to do with the dog and, as their marriage disintegrated, Mandrake found him-self without any supervision. "Basically," Johnson con-fessed, "the old boy just grew up by himself."

Johnson explained that over the last six months Man-drake had become more and more aggressive, so he decided to put his dog in the backyard, sort of an Elba for this canine Napoleon. Mandrake now lived completely outdoors, hav-ing taken command of the backyard. Johnson's housekeeper was so terrified of the dog she just threw food out to him in the yard.

I asked Johnson if he would show me Mandrake.

In a few minutes I found myself in the backyard looking at a scene as chaotic as the one in the study. Deck chairs were shredded. A tablecloth had been ripped apart. The yard was gutted with large holes.

As I was surveying this damage I spotted Mandrake. He was a handsome Manchester terrier, of moderate size, with the long, narrow head and small ears of his breed. As I watched Mandrake busily digging yet another hole with his powerful paws, his jet black and mahogany coat glistening in the afternoon sun, I remembered why these dogs were known as Manchesters. Several hundred years ago, the Manchester district of England was a center for two "poor-men's sports"—rat killing and rabbit coursing. These ter-riers were valued not for their attractiveness, but for their determined pursuit of these creatures.

Suddenly, Mandrake spotted us. He started to charge, barking furiously. We raced back into the house, as Johnson slammed the kitchen door in Mandrake's face.

"Well, McSoley," said Mr. Johnson as he tried to catch his breath, "I'm asking you again, what are you going to do about Mandrake?"

"Mr. Johnson," I replied, "I have to tell you that I have a set of seven rules that every owner needs to follow and I'm afraid that you've broken nearly every one. In particular, YOU MUST BE THE LEADER, AND THE DOG THE FOLLOWER. Mandrake is obviously out of control. By putting him in the backyard you've only increased his aggressiveness. He's the lord of the jungle out there. It's a dangerous situation, because if he breaks loose he could seriously hurt someone."

"So, McSoley, what are my options here?" said Johnson.

"I'm afraid there's not much I can recommend. Normally I'd work with you to regain control of Mandrake. But considering the amount of traveling you do, I don't see how we can structure the dog enough to gain control over him."

Johnson looked down at his shoes for a moment and said, "Well, I'm not putting him to sleep."

"I'm not suggesting that. I think I can find a home for him. But you have to make the decision."

Johnson became very sober as he thought about what I proposed. He said quietly, "I'm sure you're right. You'll help me find him a good home, McSoley."

I assured Mr. Johnson that I would. In fact, in a short time I found an owner who loved terriers and was glad to devote the time necessary to gain control of Mandrake. He and I worked with Mandrake, following the methods that will be outlined in this chapter. Mandrake became a wonderful dog, happy and content with a family that created a structured environment for him.

Several months after my visit with Johnson he called me from an airport to find out how Mandrake was doing. I assured him that Mandrake was coming along fine. "That's damn good, McSoley," he said, his voice shaking slightly. "If you see him soon, just tell him hello for me."

I've told you this story because I want you to understand that the problem of aggressive dogs usually begins with the owner and it is the owner's responsibility to deal with it. If owners neglect structuring their dog's environment like Johnson did, they are headed for serious trouble. And the emotional loss can be considerable, as I'll discuss later. Even a tough cookie like Johnson was torn up by what was the only humane and fair decision to make.

Let's look at how dogs like Mandrake get aggressive and the different kinds of aggressive behavior there are.

HOW DOGS BECOME AGGRESSIVE

Here's a pattern I've found among owners who have aggressive dogs. The problem begins when the dog is a puppy. Around six months of age, puppies start barking and become territorial. Owners praise their pup, happy he's developing into a good watch dog.

These owners rarely bring their pup in contact with other dogs or people. They limit Bozo to the property so he'll be a better protector. Unknown to them, however, they're conditioning hostility toward the world and increasing the dog's instinct to be territorial. He'll soon stop at nothing to protect his area.

The owner's unconscious conditioning continues in many small ways. When a stranger comes to the door Bozo barks and the owner rewards him by saying, "That's a good dog. You're doing a good job." Time passes. Now whenever someone comes to the door—whether stranger, friend, or relative—the dog barks. The dog is becoming more and more aggressive. The owner starts holding Bozo by the collar when someone approaches because he is afraid the dog might snap. Yet as he holds the dog he pats him on the head saying, "That's a good dog. Calm down, it's Uncle Billy." The owner is giving the dog mixed signals. The collar is on for restraint, but the dog is getting praise and affection. The dog thinks, "My master likes it when I bark. I like it when he pats me. I must be behaving properly by showing my aggression." The next step often goes like this. One day the owner leaves the front door open. The next-door neighbor comes over to borrow some sugar and the dog attacks and bites her.

The owner is afraid. When someone comes to the house, he might isolate Bozo, dragging him down the cellar or into another room. Or he might hit the dog. These methods don't work. Usually they just increase the dog's aggressiveness and may direct it toward the owner, visitors, or both. Owners become increasingly worried about the dog.

This is when I am usually brought in. Owners love their dog, but are afraid the dog might do serious harm to them or someone else. At this point I carefully devise a program to deal with the three main types of aggressive behavior—guarding, threshold, and yard. In this next section, I want to talk about each problem and the best ways for dealing with them.

OBJECT GUARDING

Several years ago I visited with a woman named Ellen who lived in New London, Connecticut. Whenever Ellen placed a hand towel down on the oven handle, Bogart, her two year old male Doberman pinscher, would grab it, run under the dining room table and guard the towel. If Ellen attempted to take the towel away Bogart would snarl viciously. Ellen had had a trainer work with the dog on obedience all summer but the problem hadn't disappeared.

When I arrived, Ellen was sitting in the living room with her daughter. After Ellen related the story of the dish towels her daughter interjected, "Ma, tell Ray about the other incidents."

Ellen demurred, saying, "It's not important."

Her daughter insisted and Ellen relented. She told me that about three weeks ago, when she bent over to give Bogart a kiss, he bit her on the breast.

Then two weeks ago, Bogart began guarding the door that led to her bedroom. If Ellen tried to get in, Bogart would growl. She became so frightened that she had taken to sleeping in the den.

As Ellen spoke, Bogart was nearby, resting quietly in the dining room. He was a good-looking dog, who outwardly seemed hardly capable of the aggressive behavior I was hearing about. I went over to Bogart. He didn't make any aggressive moves, although he was clearly sizing me up. I put him through the fundamentals—sit, stay, come, heel—which he performed well. The trainer had obviously done a good job.

I was convinced that in addition to continuing the fundamentals, I had to use a device that had proved effective in many similar cases.

I told Ellen I wanted to let Bogart attack the dish towel again because that had initiated his sense of leadership in the relationship. When he grabbed the towel I was going to use a small boat horn to startle him, so he'd make an unpleasant association between the towel and the horn's noise. I've had success with it 99 percent of the time where the owner followed my instructions. I consider it a great breakthrough in dealing with guarding behavior.

Ellen looked at me skeptically but agreed to try what I proposed. She went to the kitchen, took out a dish towel, and placed it on the oven handle. I positioned myself to the side of the kitchen entryway to watch. Bogart looked at us curiously, but when he saw Ellen put the towel on the door handle he slowly moved into the kitchen.

Bogart paused for a moment in front of the kitchen table, then leaped and snatched the towel in one swift motion. He raced back under the dining room table. Before he could begin shredding the towel I quietly approached to within 3 feet of him. Behind my back was the boat horn. Bogart stared at me, the towel firmly in his jaws. I said firmly, "No!" and immediately followed with a blast on the horn. BLAAAP—that shattering noise. Bogart leaped up, slamming his head into the table's bottom, and dropping the towel from his mouth. He ran into the living room, obviously stunned by the sound of the horn.

Ellen said excitedly, "Ray, I can't believe what I just saw—" I placed my finger to my mouth. I wanted quiet so as not to distract Bogart.

I asked Ellen to repeat the exercise. She went over to

the piano and picked up the towel. She walked into the kitchen and put the towel on the handle again. Bogart eyed us uneasily. I continued to talk calmly to Ellen. Bogart started toward the kitchen again, looking back and forth from me to the towel. He edged close to the handle. He gave me another look, and then headed for the towel. Just as his mouth was on it, I repeated, "No!" and squeezed the horn. BLAAAP. His mouth flew open, his eyes bulged out. He raced to a corner of the living room and lay down, completely shaken. He didn't attempt to take the towel again.

This was exactly the reaction I wanted. I asked Ellen to use the horn every time Bogart put the towel in his mouth, and to call me in a few days and tell me if his guarding behavior had stopped. I also had her continue the program of structuring she had begun with her trainer.

Sure enough, in a week Ellen called to tell me the horn had worked. There had been only one incident with the towel. Ellen used the horn and Bogart dropped the towel immediately. There also had been no other incidents of aggressive behavior.

The key to using the horn effectively is making sure the dog makes the association between the object being guarded—shoes, clothes, eyeglasses—and the noise from the horn. The best way to do this is to let the dog go near the object that he wants to take and just as he is about to snatch it in his mouth, tell him "No!" and *immediately follow* by blasting the horn, which should be kept out of sight, usually behind the owner's back.

The larger question is why do dogs guard objects? What normally occurs is that a dog picks up an object, perhaps the owner's glasses because it has the owner's smell on them, and runs with it. The owner thinks this is cute and laughs instead of remaining neutral until the dog drops the object. The dog now knows this is a great way to get attention. So the dog continues to pick up the same object and the game gets more serious. The owner may try to bribe the dog with a food treat, which, of course, is just reinforcing the dog for guarding behavior. When this trick doesn't work, the owner becomes annoyed and yells at the dog. The dog growls back and nothing is resolved. In the next encounter

I'm about to use the boat horn to stop this laundry robber.

over a snatched object the owner may hit the dog. The dog growls louder, or threatens to bite. At this point the owner usually backs away. The dog soon learns that he can cope with the owner by acting aggressively. Now the problem is severe. The dog is definitely in the leader position.

I remember a couple, Hal and Dotty, who lived in Sudbury, a graceful suburb of Boston, with a magnificent Lhasa Apso named Tai Pai. It seemed that Tai Pai had one particular object he liked to guard—ladies' panties. Tai Pai would grab Dotty's panties and run around the house and bite his owners if they attempted to take them back.

One night, Hal and Dotty, who entertained frequently for business purposes, had a couple, Herb and Janet, over as weekend guests. As the two couples were sitting in the living room, in strolled Tai Pai with Janet's panties firmly in his mouth. Janet had left her suitcase open and Tai Pai had rummaged through until he found the panties. Hal and Dotty apologized profusely as they chased Tai Pai around the house trying to grab the panties back. The next morning they called me. The boat horn did the trick.

Object guarding is a difficult problem because if the owner attempts to reach for the object the dog will bite. Even if the owners begin to teach the dog the structuring fundamentals, it's not unusual for the problem to persist. I've found that the best method for dealing with this problem is the horn.

THRESHOLD AGGRESSION

Threshold aggression—dogs who are aggressive in certain parts of the house or when someone is coming into the house—is one of the major problems I see in my travels.

There are degrees of this problem. Dogs who run to the door and bark as a warning to the owner pose no overt threat. Dogs who bark and indicate more aggressive posturing— perhaps showing their teeth—could bite. Dogs who might bite at the threshold, but who, instead, calm down once they see that the owner is relaxed and hear the pleasant voice tone of the visitor are less likely to bite once the visitor is seated and relaxed.

But when a dog is aggressive at the threshold and senses his owner is on guard, nervous, or angry with a visitor he can explode at any moment.

This happened once right before my eyes on my first visit with a young woman named Sabrina who had been having problems with her one-hundred-pound German shepherd named Hans. We were in her kitchen talking about Hans, who was lying quietly beside her, when her kitchen doorbell rang.

Sabrina went to the door, opened it partially and spoke with a deliveryman who had a package for her. He asked Sabrina to sign his invoice slip. As they talked, Hans got up and walked over to Sabrina, just as she was opening the door so she could sign the invoice. As Sabrina started to write her name, I saw a look of shock cross the delivery-man's face. He took a step back. In that instant, Hans leaped straight at him, tearing into his arms and legs, knocking him down the steps into the driveway.

I sprang out of my chair and ran outside. The delivery-man was on the ground, his arms up around his face, trying to protect himself. I grabbed Hans by the tail, lifting his hind legs off the ground and dragging him back into the house. The deliveryman was bleeding in several places. I took him to a nearby hospital. Although he was shaken up badly he wasn't seriously hurt.

Later that day when I returned to talk to Sabrina about Hans, she admitted that this was not the first biting incident. Hans had attacked a diaper deliveryman and had put seven stitches into a babysitter's ear when she was playing tug-of-war with him. Sabrina told me she had been afraid to call me because she thought I'd recommend that the dog be put to sleep.

Unfortunately, Sabrina wasn't the first client who confessed that her dog had bitten a number of people before she called me. Owners should address this problem behavior immediately before their dog seriously harms someone. Owners become frozen by their fear of losing the animal. There are, however, solutions other than putting the dog to sleep.

The two techniques that work the best are *distraction* and *going to his place*. I prefer distraction because it usually takes less time for the dog to learn. Some owners find it difficult because it requires them to act happy even when they are anxious.

Here's how it works. Have a family member come to the door but not ring the doorbell. As Dad comes through the door, get a ball or Frisbee and start a game with your dog. Throw the ball against a wall or down the hall and have Rover retrieve it. Then open the door and let Dad in. When the dog returns, exclaim "Good dog" and introduce Dad to your dog in a cheerful voice. What you're doing is teaching your dog to associate someone coming in with a happy, not frightening, situation. You are *switch conditioning* him out of his aggressive mood. I want family members used here because they tend to come through the backdoor; strangers, friends, and relatives come through the front door.

After you've done this for a few days, start to ring the doorbell, which is usually used when people come to the home. Then enlist the aid of friends and neighbors to play this game with the dog.

Practice switch conditioning twice a day. Each session should consist of three to six throws. At a minimum you want your dog to put his mouth around the ball or, at least, to run after the ball. Say "Good dog" when he accomplishes either activity.

After about two weeks of this exercise, begin the game under normal circumstances. If your spouse or friend comes over and rings the doorbell, immediately start to play the game. It's important now to get your dog to put the ball in his mouth. A dog in a fun mood is far less likely to be aggressive.

After you have done this for a while, try the game when strangers come to the door. This is the true test. If it works, you have created an activity that should eliminate the problem of your dog threatening people.

Remember, take this one step at a time. Don't be impatient. This is a very effective technique and it in no way impedes your dog's ability to protect you or watch the house. If you feel threatened by someone, your dog will pick your fear up quickly and become aggressive. He will also still be aggressive when someone is trying to break into the house, because it's his territory. All I'm doing is changing his attitude in *your* presence.

The other method of dealing with an aggressive dog is to have him go to his place. Here the owner commands his dog to return to an area far away from the door. At the beginning, it will be necessary to bring the dog to his place and then command "Stay" and walk back toward the door. When he does, reward the dog with high praise, "That's a good dog."

The same step-by-step approach of ball playing should

be used here. First try it with no bell ringing. Next have someone ring the bell. Both exercises should be done twice a day, three to six times, for about a week. Then command "Go to your place" when your spouse or friends come to the door. Finally, try it when strangers ring the bell.

This technique puts physical distance between the person at the door and the dog, which is very important, and calms down the dog and owner. This method works best when owners feel at ease being very dominant with the dog. It may require more personality adjustment than simply playing ball with the dog.

Try first one, then the other. See what works best for you and be consistent.

AGGRESSION IN THE YARD

Here's a scenario. In a yard bounded by a chain-link fence sits a four-month-old puppy named Cookie. Every day three people walk by—two children and a businesswoman. They walk by in the morning and in the evening. Cookie watches as they go by.

Time passes. Cookie is now six months old and she starts to bark as the three people pass back and forth.

At nine months Cookie is barking and running along the fence.

On Cookie's first birthday her owner forgets to close the gate. Cookie spots the little boy and girl. Out she races and starts to attack them, biting them on the arms and legs. The owner is thunderstruck. "I can't believe Cookie did this. She's such a good dog."

What happened? In the owner's mind all she did was put her dog outside. But, in fact, what she did was to subject Cookie to *one year of frustration*. Barrier frustration. Cookie wanted the three people to pay attention to her, maybe pet her. Day after day, the chain fence prevented Cookie from reaching them. All along the fence was her territory. When the gate was open, Cookie attacked.

If Cookie's owner understood a little dog training she'd

have realized she had unknowingly created a situation called agitation. When German shepherd dogs are being trained for protection, aggressiveness is increased in a simple way. The dog stands beside the trainer. Behind them an "agitator" claps his hands. The dog turns to look and the agitator runs off. The trainer says "That's a good dog." This action is repeated. Eventually the dog starts to bark. As this continues, he becomes more aggressive. Finally, the trainer has the dog biting the heavy sleeve of the agitator.

That's exactly what's happened in our scenario. The three people who walked by served as unpaid agitators. Day after day their presence increased Cookie's aggressiveness.

I saw an interesting example of this kind of conditioning several years ago. A woman named Andrea Graham called me to complain about Lucy, her bull mastiff who had become very aggressive in the backyard. I arrived the next afternoon. I spotted Lucy sitting in the yard and decided to say hello. I approached her from the right-hand side of the chain-link fence. Lucy started to bark violently. She did indeed seem to be very aggressive.

I went inside and talked with Andrea, who told me that Lucy had become very violent outside in recent months. I asked her to bring Lucy inside. When Andrea opened the porch door, Lucy raced in, and within a few minutes she and I were good friends.

I asked Andrea to let me outside with Lucy because I wanted to see her behavior in the yard. Lucy ran outside and was playing happily when she suddenly started to bark. Then I saw why. In the distance I spotted three golfers approaching a tee. (This house was situated near a golf course.) As they teed up, Lucy's barking became louder. The golfers were the unpaid agitators! Day after day they strode in front of the dog and then walked away—in her mind—when she started barking!

Owners believe they're doing good when they let their dog into the yard. They think he's getting fresh air and plenty of exercise chasing squirrels and birds. But if you let your dog out for long periods of time, you're creating a situation that will lead him to become aggressive and territorial.

So don't leave your dog outside for long periods of time; over one hour should never be allowed. If he has become aggressive, then basic commands have to be drilled home. As in all forms of aggressiveness, ultimately you have to regain the leadership position in the relationship or more troublesome behavior will occur.

A FINAL TRIP

The hardest part of my job is when I have to tell an owner his dog must be put to sleep. Although I've had to do it dozens of times over the years, it has never gotten easy.

A short time ago I was called in to work with Bofie, a large, four-year-old Bernese mountain dog. Bofie's problem was that he'd become very aggressive as soon as he got into his owner's car and golf cart. I spoke at length with his owners, Jim and Betty, and I couldn't find a particular reason for Bofie's behavior—he was, in general, well trained and a kind dog. I decided to work on the fundamentals with Bofie so as to really fine-tune his responses to his owners' commands.

Bofie did well over the four months I was with him. I started to work him in a golf cart. I'd put Bofie inside and I'd say, "Bofie, out," and he'd leap out. After a while he was becoming pretty good. Then I brought him to his owners' car and was working the same command with increasing success.

One Sunday night after I'd been out on the boat with Mary and the kids I got a call from Jim. Bofie had gone into their car early Saturday morning and wouldn't come out. He was threatening anyone who'd come close. I went over immediately.

When I got near the car Bofie began snarling viciously. I opened the car door cautiously and commanded, "Bofie, out." Bofie didn't move and continued to bark. I tried again. "Bofie, out." This time he moved slowly out of the car, growling as he came near me. I said "Sit," which he did immediately, but he remained agitated for a few more minutes. I took him by the collar and tied him to the back-steps rail while I went in to talk with Betty and Jim.

I told them that Bofie had a dark side to his personality, something that made him suddenly become so vicious. I recommended that he be put to sleep. Betty became upset and said to me, "Ray, we'll just not ever put Bofie in the car." I said that was impossible; there had to be times Bofie had to go in a car—to the vet, or when he was boarded if they went on a trip. More importantly, I couldn't promise them Bofie's anger wouldn't be triggered by something else. Their lives, or their neighbors, could be endangered. Finally, the message sank in. Betty and Jim agreed. I volunteered to take Bofie to the Angell Memorial Animal Hospital.

It seemed like a long ride to the hospital, even though it was no more than half an hour away. Bofie rode beside me, and as could be expected, was calm throughout, making it that much harder to do what I knew had to be done. Bofie stared out through the passenger side window most of the time, the small brass bell that hung from his green nylon dog collar clanging gently.

At the hospital I brought Bofie into the side room where I see patients with behavioral problems and went to get a doctor. I returned a few minutes later with Dr. Dean Vicksman, a good friend of mine. I helped the doctor put Bofie up on the table. I put my right hand on Bofie's head to hold him still and with my left hand I scratched him behind his ears. Dr. Vicksman inserted the needle into Bofie's right front foreleg, and after a few seconds Bofie slumped on the table, gradually losing consciousness. Moments later he passed on. I couldn't stop my petting behind his ear until Dr. Vicksman put his hand over mine and said, "Ray, it's over." Gently, I took off Bofie's collar and bell. I wanted to bring it back to Jim and Betty.

Unfortunately, I know in my travels I'll be meeting more Bofies. Dogs who go over an edge where even I can't bring them back. Every dog owner who has to face this most difficult of all decisions has my sympathy and my respect. I, more than anyone, know how you feel.

CHAPTER

7

Housesoiling

ALAN Stone was trying to make himself understood: "You're treading on thin ice, Duke."

Alan's eleven-and-a-half-month-old Samoyed, who was running down the street, stopped near a street lamp, ready to relieve himself.

Alan walked quickly toward Duke saying, "That's right Duke, go." But as soon as Alan came near him, Duke darted down the steps of a street-level apartment.

Alan shouted, "You won't get away, now."

Moments later, man and dog emerged, Duke now firmly leashed. Alan dragged his dog over to the street lamp and pleaded once more, "Go, Duke. Come on, boy . . . go."

Duke just stared at Alan, straining to get away from the lamp. Alan turned to me and said, "What I'd tell you, two hours wasted. No matter how hard I try, no matter how patient I'm with him, he won't go outside!"

A short time later, we were sitting in the comfortable living room of Alan's apartment. Duke was lying down beside his master, calmly chewing on a rubber hamburger, as Alan gently petted him. The affection between them was obvious, and Alan's behavior far more in keeping with a man whose occupation was a classical music disc jockey.

But Alan was frustrated, unable to understand why he couldn't get Duke to relieve himself outside.

"Mr. McSoley, the last nine months have been a nightmare. I take Duke out for hours at a time. I walk him all over the city of Boston and he never goes. I get back here and as soon as I'm not looking he goes. I can't stand it anymore. All of this after I used the rapid housebreaking method."

"The what method?" I said.

"The rapid housebreaking method. I'm sure you've heard of it. A friend said it was foolproof. He told me the first three days you have a puppy you have to devote complete attention to him. Every time the puppy starts to go you take him by the neck, give him a slight slap on the rear end, put his face in the poop and yell at him. Then you bring the dog outside. So the first weekend I had Duke I sat in the kitchen for hours watching him. And every time he started to go—Pow! A single shot in the rear. Then I'd take him outside for a walk. But Duke has never figured it out. I guess he's just a stupid dog."

Alan was wrong. Duke was not a stupid dog; he simply didn't understand that he was supposed to go outside. Alan was the one with the problem, because after nine months of failure he didn't have the slightest idea that the rapid housebreaking method was completely worthless and that everything he was doing was reinforcing Duke's inability to go outside.

Alan had completely broken my rule number one— YOU MUST BE RESPONSIBLE FOR LEARNING HOW TO COMMUNICATE WITH YOUR DOG. In Duke's mind, what he had been learning as Alan gave him "a single shot" was that he would get punished for going. The dog didn't understand that the punishment was for *where* he was going. Whenever Alan took Duke outside he never let him out of his sight. Duke therefore would never go. He wasn't going to get hit again if he could help it.

Since Duke wouldn't go, Alan would get more and more frustrated each time they went out. Alan's anxiety and yelling would only reinforce Duke's fear, ensuring that he would never go. But as soon as Duke got home, and Alan left him alone, he would go. He was safe.

Alan made three major mistakes when it came to teaching Duke about housesoiling. First, Alan was convinced that the method of teaching he was using was correct. Alan was not a brutal man; he did not hit his dog to hurt him. He simply thought he was doing the right thing for his dog. Secondly, Alan projected his feelings onto the dog. Alan thought, "Well if somebody hit me every time I'd start to go inside, I would make up my mind to go outside." But that is not how his dog thought. Finally, Alan's ego was involved. Like many owners he blamed the dog—Duke was stupid. It couldn't possibly be anything Alan was doing.

I explained all this to Alan and then outlined a program I had found to be most effective in dealing with housesoiling.

The first step was for Alan to stop punishing the dog. It was not working and only helping condition a nervous, frightened dog.

I also told Alan he would have to work on the fundamentals—sit, come, stay, and proper heeling. Alan had to gain control over Duke. The dog's racing outside and Alan's chasing him clearly indicated that there was precious little structuring going on.

Then I told Alan that Duke had to be placed on a strict feeding schedule. Alan was a big man, and fairly overweight. He fed Duke some of the food he ate during the day. That had to stop immediately. Instead, Alan had to feed Duke only at eight o'clock in the morning and at six o'clock at night. This would help cut down the number of times Duke had to go and it would put some time limits into their relationship. I then told Alan that he would have to buy regular suppositories at a drug store. At night he should take Duke into his bedroom with him and tie him with a short line to the bedpost. Almost all dogs hate to mess in their own territory so it was unlikely that Duke would do anything at night.

Alan would have to get up at 6:30 and give the dog a suppository. Then he should take the dog for a walk. The suppository would force Duke to go and, as he was, Alan was to say in a happy voice, "Good dog, Duke. That's a good dog." Then he would have to repeat this procedure at night.

Alan looked a little glum after I finished outlining my plan. I asked him what was the matter.

"I . . . I have to give him a suppository?"

"I'm afraid so. It's the only way we can get Duke to start going in front of you."

Alan reluctantly agreed to try. I told him to call me the next morning.

At 7:15 A.M., I picked up the phone to hear Alan say excitedly, "You were right, Mr. McSoley—Duke went outside. Boy was he shaking. But he went. I kept saying, 'That's a good boy.' And he did. It was great."

Within three weeks Duke was going outside without trauma.

HOUSETRAINING COMMON SENSE

Like Alan, most owners are punishing their dogs for going in the *wrong* place rather than rewarding the pup for eliminating in the *right* place. Your dog wants more than anything else to please you, and given the proper cues will do the correct behavior. What many owners cannot understand is that their dog isn't soiling their house because he's angry, stubborn, or stupid. The pup simply isn't housetrained.

Here are the three different types of housesoiling dilemmas:

- The naive dog
- The insecure dog
- The submissive/excited urinator

Let's first talk about the naive dog. The owner hasn't conditioned the pup to understand that going outside is okay, and that pooping and peeing inside is unacceptable. By my definition, the dog who goes outside is trained; the one who goes inside (or both inside and outside), against the owner's wishes, isn't trained. There isn't any middle ground.

Here's how you housetrain the naive dog.

- Think that you're training the dog from day one
- Establish the proper area outside
- Use a "keying" phrase and proper praise
- Set up a strict feeding and out schedule
- Use proper confinement techniques
- Establish a proper sleeping area
- Keep a daily chart
- Utilize an effective odor neutralizer and properly clean a soiled area
- Structure your dog daily
- Check with your vet
- Punish effectively when necessary
- Take lots of patience pills

Let's go through each of these instructions.

Think That You're Training Your Dog From Day One

No matter what he's done to your house in the past, it's best for you mentally to wipe the slate clean in terms of anger and guilt. Give yourself a break and start off the training with a positive attitude.

Establish the Proper Area Outside

Where do you want the pup to go? That's where you bring the dog. I suggest, if at all possible, the backyard. The one exception to fixating on a proper area is when you're working with a dog who's having a hard time figuring out that you want him outside. In that case, I don't care what part of the yard he goes in at first, just as long as he goes. After a while, you can try to get him to a spot in the yard.

Use a "Keying" Phrase and Proper Praise

A "begging" phrase very important aspect of proper conditioning. I use "Hurry up" with Jake. My breeder and friend Mimi Kearney uses "Into the woods" with her retrievers, who go to the woods behind her house. Do not use a phrase like "Good dog."

Here's how keying works. Whenever I took Jake outside for him to eliminate, as soon as he began to eliminate, I'd say, five or six times, "Hurry up, Hurry up." As soon as Jake finished I'd say, "Good dog, atta boy," and I'd bring him back into the house. What I was doing was conditioning Jake to understand that the primary reason for him to be outside in the backyard was to eliminate. After you give your dog exercise in the morning, bring him back in the house for five minutes and then go outside to the backyard for him to do his duty.

Your dog will go quickly wherever he is because he's learned to associate the keying phrase with eliminating. There are many times when Jake is with me for the day in the car and I'm racing from one client to the next and I only have a couple of minutes for him to stop and eliminate. I tell him "Hurry up" and he goes fast, with no sniffing for ten minutes to find just the right spot.

Set Up a Strict Feeding and Out Schedule

What goes in comes out. If you feed Bozo one day at 8:00 A.M. and the next at 10:30 A.M., don't expect him to defecate on any type of schedule. When the pup's fully housetrained and you want to feed him on a self-feeding basis you have my permission. Until then, feed him on a schedule. For example, for three feedings a day, you might feed:

> 7:00 A.M.–7:30 A.M. (pick up dish after thirty minutes)
> 1:00 P.M.–1:30 P.M. (pick up dish after thirty minutes)
> 7:00 P.M.–7:30 P.M. (pick up dish after thirty minutes)

No water after 8:00 P.M.

Also establish a regime for taking the pup out, every day at the same time, including the weekends. It does no good to take the dog out ten times on the weekend and twice during the week. Be consistent.

Bozo sitting near a food table. No extra treats!

Use Proper Confinement Techniques

I like crate training (see pages 146–47). It's foolish to allow your dog to run helter-skelter through your house if he has no sense of where to eliminate. If you use a crate, be fair with your dog. Don't expect the pup to live in the crate for long periods of time.

Establish a Proper Sleeping Area

When housetraining, I tell my clients to have their dogs sleep in their bedrooms. Either put Bozo in a crate, or tie

him on a short line (sixteen inches) to the foot of your bed.
I don't want the dog on your bed.

Keep a Daily Chart

Here's what a good chart looks like:

	What	When	Where	Comments
MONDAY				
	Pooped/ peed	7:15 A.M.	Backyard	
	Peed	9:30 A.M.	Backyard	
	Peed	11:00 A.M.	Dining room	
	Pooped	2:30 P.M.	Backyard	
	Peed	4:20 P.M.	Backyard	
	Pooped	6:15 P.M.	Kitchen	Was standing at the door
	Pooped/ peed	11:00 P.M.	Backyard	

The chart is a marvelous aid for the owner. It gives you
a good picture of what's going on with the pup. No person's
memory is good enough to remember who did what and
where on a daily basis. The chart enables you to do this
with consistency. It will tell you what type of pattern, if
any, the dog is following. It will also tell you whether things
are getting better, getting worse, or remaining status quo.
I require my clients with housesoiling problems to keep a
daily chart.

Utilize an Effective Odor Neutralizer and Properly Clean a Soiled Area

There are a host of neutralizers on the market; some work,
some don't. If you select one that works, fine; if not, I

suggest using either a mixture of one half white vinegar and one half warm water (mix up to fifty or sixty gallons at a time!) or else plain old club soda straight. What you want to do is neutralize the pH factor in the urine. When you see a spot, first blot up the urine as dry as possible. Second, saturate the area with the neutralizer. Third, blot that up as thoroughly as possible. If you don't neutralize the area, then the pup will more than likely return to the scene of the crime.

Never, never use ammonia! It's like a magnet to a nail for a dog.

And *never, never* clean up a soiled area with Bozo present. If you do, you'll be making clean-up a high point in his day.

Structure Your Dog Daily

You know the reasons by now. An unstructured dog may make any place his toilet area because no limits and authority have been established.

Check with Your Vet

You can use all the fancy modification techniques you want, but if Bozo has a physical problem that contributes to his eliminating in the house and you neglect it, he's going to continue.

Punish Effectively When Necessary

You don't housetrain a dog by punishing him for going in the wrong place; you reward him for going in the right place. However, if you see the pup going on the family Oriental, then tell him "No!" firmly and shoo him from the room and clean it up.

There's one exception to this procedure. When Jake was about four and a half months he began to poop in the living room, in one certain area. He did it for three days in a row.

On the third day, after spotting the mess, I went to Jake, quietly brought him to the living room, and tied him on a line as close to the mess as possible, about one foot away. I then left the room. After fifteen minutes I reentered the room, walked over to Jake, and scolded him, "Bad dog, bad dog." Then I left. After another fifteen minutes I entered the room again and repeated "Bad dog" and let him off the line. He shot out of the room and I cleaned up the mess. Jake never pooped there again.

Keep punishment to a minimum. Don't lose your temper and yell and hit the pup. That doesn't solve the problem.

Take Lots of Patience Pills

This is self-explanatory. Teaching housetraining just takes time. So keep at it until Bozo learns.

HOUSETRAINING THE INSECURE DOG

The insecure dog may urinate inside. The urination may be expressed through simply urinating, or a male dog may begin marking. That is, you may begin to notice the corners of walls, the legs of tables, the lower sections of curtains drenched or spotted with urine. Some female dogs mark by leglifting as well as males, but it's not the norm. If your male is marking inside, and he's intact, I would strongly advise your neutering him as soon as possible. The problem may be hormones and not insecurity.

However, if this is done and the problem continues, then you have an insecure animal, one who is attempting to deal with this feeling by marking territory. A crisis in Bozo's life, such as moving, a new piece of furniture, a renovation, the departure of a son or daughter, or other similar type of event, may result in a marking problem.

The solution to this problem is in eliminating insecurity through structuring. Two to three short, five-minute structure sessions daily (particularly in those rooms where he's marking), coupled with eliminating overindulgence toward the pet, give him a better understanding of where he is in the pecking order. When he's more aware of his place, he becomes more secure, feeling less need to mark his dwelling.

Don't punish your dog for marking. It will be counterproductive to solving the problem, as it will make him more insecure than he is already.

THE SUBMISSIVE/EXCITED URINATOR

When I owned Kate, my wonderful yellow Lab, she would greet me when I returned home by urinating. I've had hundreds of clients with this kind of housesoiling problem and I tell them the same thing—ignore the behavior, and ignore the dog.

Here's how to do this. When you return home, completely ignore the dog, including eye contact. Allow the dog to calm down, which may take a few minutes. Then in another room, bend down, perhaps even facing away from the pup. When the dog comes over, pet Bozo *under* the chin, not on the top of the head. Begin looking at the dog after thirty seconds or so.

I completely ignored Kate this way, and, after a month, she stopped peeing when she saw me come through the door.

All three types of housesoiling can be difficult to deal with and to control. I want you to take your time and follow my instructions. After a while, you should see major improvement in your beloved pet.

CHAPTER

8

Phobias

PICTURE this. A family named the Beisers, living in Wayland, Mass., father Marty, mother Kathy, children Caitlin and Michael, went off to a football game, leaving their beautiful four-year-old golden retriever, Jessie, alone. Jessie is terribly phobic during thunderstorms, but fortunately, someone always had been home during a storm. Over the years, the family had learned to check the weather forecast carefully before departing on family outings.

On this particular afternoon, however, a freak thunderstorm struck just as the game ended. The family raced back to their home worried about Jessie. As the Beisers pulled near their house they beheld an amazing scene—their next-door neighbors Arthur and Ann Lubow and their two girls Nadia and Erica were heaving apples at the Beisers' second-floor bedroom window, where their lovely golden sat ready to jump. (Since it was a warm fall day the Beisers had left the window open.) Jessie had become so scared by the storm that she had slammed out the window screen in a desperate attempt to escape. The neighbors' ingenuity had saved the day. Every time Jessie would show her face in the window ready to jump, the Lubows would throw apples.

Phobias—a persistent abnormal fear of something—are

one of the most difficult behavioral problems I deal with; the most severe ones are capable of endangering the life of a dog, as was the case with Jessie. There are mild phobias, such as when the dog demonstrates fear of a vacuum cleaner and merely stays out of a room while it's being vacuumed. And there are extreme phobias where dogs—during thunderstorms or when they hear loud noises—are compelled to get out from wherever they are even if it means jumping off a building.

There are four kinds of fears: of noises, of people, of places, of objects. I want to deal with each in turn. But before I do, I want to talk about why dogs become phobic.

ORIGINS OF PHOBIAS

The origins of a dog's fear may be genetic. If so, it is important to talk with the breeder and to find out what the personalities of the mother and father were like. This should be done before the dog is purchased, but at whatever time, always check with your breeder to see if this pattern of behavior is found in the dog's family. For example, if you're purchasing a dog for hunting, you don't want a pup that's linked genetically to gun shyness.

Early environmental factors, however, can profoundly affect a dog's behavior.

In the early developmental stages of a puppy's life, around the eighth through tenth week a puppy enters into a fear-imprinting period during which exposure to loud noises may cause him to become fearful for the rest of his life. Furthermore, puppies who aren't exposed to people by age thirteen weeks will be fearful of humans. They can have an almost catatonic reaction when exposed to humans and are thus unsuitable as companions. Their ability to adapt to households is very stunted. Any human contact during those six to thirteen weeks diminishes that extreme state.

Several years ago I worked with an eleven-week-old puppy that had received no human contact prior to coming to the home of the owner. I could take the pup and put her in the middle of the room, walk away and sit on the other side for twenty minutes and the puppy wouldn't move. Since I knew I had a real problem in the making I acted quickly to break down the fear. I started basic structuring and I used a great deal of food reward to get the pup to open up to me and respond to my commands. Of course, I recommend, as you'll see in Chapter 12 on puppies, that owners avoid buying dogs with these kinds of problems unless they're willing to devote a great deal of time and energy to the pup.

PHOBIAS OF SOUND

Prevention as always is the best way to deal with phobias. When I talked with Jessie's owners, they told me that Jessie was nervous during thunderstorms when she was just a puppy, as early as six months. What did they do to handle the problem? They said that they would try to calm her down. How did they do this? Kathy said, "Marty and I would call Jessie to us, tell her it was all right and pat her. We'd do it every time." Wrong, wrong, wrong. What Marty and Kathy were doing was not helping Jessie over her phobia but rather reinforcing it.

Never attempt to reassure a dog during a period of anxiety by talking soothingly to him and petting him. You should only reassure the dog when he's doing the right behavior.

If you have a dog that is phobic and he is comfortable in the bathtub during a storm then that might be the best place for him. Or he might prefer a dark closet. If he feels secure there and the problem never gets worse than that, then it might be best to let him alone. But if the problem is more substantial here's what you need to do.

When you see your dog foaming at the mouth during a thunderstorm or when he hears loud noises such as firecrackers you should *switch condition* the dog. Grab his ball and immediately begin playing with him. Be as spontaneous and upbeat as you can possibly be. The idea here is twofold:

first to switch his mood from one of anxiety to one of fun, and second, to push the thunder into the background. What you're doing is making the primary focus of the dog the ball playing. It doesn't have to be ball playing, as long as it's fun. Just don't inadvertently reinforce Bozo's being phobic.

Bozo may respond immediately to the ball playing, which is terrific. If he doesn't, don't give up. Keep trying. If he even shows the slightest interest in the ball, make a big deal out of it. Laugh, clap your hands. Follow the biblical injunction—make a joyous noise.

Desensitization

Some animal behavioral scientists have developed a method of treating phobias known as desensitization. A similar technique is used on humans who are phobic. Under the guidance of a therapist, a person is put into a relaxed state and then helped to imagine progressively more fear-producing renditions of the phobia while maintaining a state of relaxation. When the person can remain relaxed while the mind reruns the fearful situation, then the phobia may be reduced or eliminated.

Although desensitization experiments with dogs in controlled scientific conditions have shown some positive results, I've had little success with this program. There may be several reasons for this. Under the best of circumstances desensitization is a long and difficult program. One must be capable of reading the dog very closely in order to monitor progress and regression. Perhaps even more problematic is the fact that the controlled environment of a scientific experiment can't be reproduced in the home.

But for those who are interested here's how to do desensitization for a dog phobic about loud noises or thunderstorms. Buy one of the tapes on the market such as *The Ultimate Storm*. Put the tape on and play it loud so you can see if your dog responds fearfully. If he does, then proceed. If he doesn't, take the tape back. You won't be able to make any progress.

If the dog responds positively, then start the program this way. Place the tape on the lowest volume level possible during the dog's feeding time. If the dog continues to eat, then the volume is acceptable. If he doesn't eat, lower the volume. After one week of this, increase the volume slightly. If the dog shows any fear, decrease the volume. After a week increase the volume again. As long as your dog tolerates the tape while eating, continue to increase the volume on a weekly basis, monitoring his behavior as you do.

How well the program works will have to wait until the next thunderstorm. In some cases, the dog will now tolerate the loud noise and remain calm. In other cases, unfortunately, the dog will exhibit a fearful response. If that happens, then I recommend not continuing with the program.

Crating

If you've tried both switch conditioning and desensitization and neither has worked, then you might attempt the following program.

Three years ago I was called to Newport, Rhode Island, to some of the most breathtaking mansions in the world. During the summer months Newport receives its share of violent squalls and accompanying severe thunderclaps. A wealthy bachelor by the name of Tom owned an eight-year-old standard poodle named Dickens who would destroy furniture during a thunderstorm. Since Tom had a fine collection of antique furniture, Dickens was costing his owner thousands of dollars in repair bills.

Because of Dickens's age I figured there was no way to switch condition him out of his behavior so I put together the following program. First, I conditioned the dog to a crate at night. Second, by employing a storm tape I got the dog to run into the crate whenever the tape was played. Third, when a thunderstorm struck, Dickens was sent into his crate and Tom rewarded him heavily through the use of food treats and praise. In the final stage of the program, the dog ran into the crate on his own whenever a storm passed over.

This was a most time-consuming program—two months, every day—for the owner. I've mentioned it because it's innovative and it worked. For many owners, simply putting the dog in a vandal-proof dog crate is the most effective solution. The crate, however, must be rugged, or the dog will chew right through it. One-inch-square wire mesh is essential. Two manufacturers who meet this criteria are Central Metal and 5Ts. I recommend crating only as a last resort.

PHOBIAS OF PEOPLE

Some dogs are afraid of people. As I said earlier, this may be related to the amount of exposure they received when they were a puppy or to the kind of treatment they received. In many cases I find the owner has also been rewarding the dog for being shy. They pat the dog when a stranger comes to the house, maybe even picking up and bringing the dog over to the stranger. Or the owner feels sorry for the dog because he's phobic and winds up overindulging the dog emotionally or in terms of rewards.

How does a shy dog act toward people? When a person comes into the house the dog avoids him, walking away to a corner of the house or the room. If the person stays and talks with the owner for about two or three minutes, and the person remains neutral, avoiding eye contact and not making any overt moves toward the dog, the dog may come over to the person. The other extreme is when a person enters the house and is neutral toward the dog, but the dog creeps away from that person, tail under his legs, looking in extreme fear. This dog never warms up, and stays hidden in a corner.

Here's what I do when I come into a home with a dog that's afraid of people. I completely ignore the dog and just talk in a natural voice to the owner. After a while the dog usually approaches me out of curiosity. I continue to ignore the dog, making *no eye contact* and concentrating on the owner. After a few minutes I drop down one hand, which the dog will soon start to sniff. I continue to make no eye contact and ignore the dog. After a few minutes I take one finger and tickle the dog under his chin, but I still don't look at him (I don't move toward the top of his head because it's more threatening). After a few more minutes I start to tickle him with all my fingers. In a couple of minutes I pull my hand back and scratch behind his ear and say quietly "Good dog." That's it for the first encounter.

Over and over clients tell me I'm the first person able to pat the dog. What I do works because I'm letting the dog find me and I don't threaten him in any way. I just calmly reassure him that I'm a friend.

The next time I come I repeat this procedure and bring a food treat with me to reward the dog for being friendly. On my visit after that I play with him a little more, gradually building up the dog's confidence and trust in me.

This is how I want your friends and strangers to act when they come to your house. Don't be afraid to ask people to do this. It's the only way you can continually reinforce Bozo for the right behavior. Gradually the dog will see strangers and neighbors as nonthreatening.

Now here's a variation on this technique. The first visit from a friend should follow the above procedure of slowly tickling under the dog's chin. On the next visit, have the friend bring with him a tennis ball. When the dog comes over, have the friend throw the ball, and say "Go fetch," but he still shouldn't make eye contact with the dog. Just toss it into a corner so Bozo can run after it. What I'm trying to accomplish here is to make the ball what I call an "intervening positive stimulus." The phobic dog after a while may identify the ball with fun. The ball will become more important than the dog's fear of the stranger.

I recently used this technique with a phobic dog named Ruggles. I threw the ball, told him "Go fetch" and Ruggles raced after the ball and ran back and forth in the living room. After a short time he dropped the ball. I picked it up and tossed it again. Ruggles galloped after it, chomped down and played with it again for a few minutes before dropping it. I went over, picked up the ball and sat down on a chair, holding the ball in one hand. Ruggles came over, sniffed the ball, then sniffed my hand. I patted him on the head and then he jumped up and licked me on my face. Ruggles's owner, Joyce, almost fell off her couch. She told me that Ruggles had never done that with anyone.

So ball throwing with a phobic dog can be a powerful variation of the basic technique.

Another way of dealing with phobic dogs is to saturate them with people by taking them to a crowded city area. I recommend this *only* if the dog can properly heel. The dog has to be under your control or you'll just be reinforcing his fear in two ways: the numbers of people will overwhelm him, and you'll undermine his confidence in you because you won't be able to control him. If you can heel him correctly, then every time Bozo wants to walk away, you'll be able to bring him back, extending your control over him and reassuring him that nothing will happen if he sees people. The dog begins to calm down because he picks up the sense of confidence in the owner. The owner *transfers* his confidence to the dog. It is this transference that helps make it effective.

PHOBIAS OF PLACES

Some dogs become fearful of walking up or down stairs. What many clients do is to start to carry or drag the dog up and down. This is useless, unless you want to use your dog in place of free weights to develop your upper body.

Here's how to deal with this phobia. Put the dog on the first step of the stairs with his leash on and you standing on the floor a short distance away. Call Bozo, "Here, boy," and apply gentle but firm pressure on the leash. If he comes, great. If he doesn't, just keep calling him and applying steady pressure until he jumps off. Then give him a ton of praise. Repeat 3 more times, then call it a day. You may give a food treat as a reward each time he succeeds.

You have to repeat this procedure all the way up the

stairs, one step at a time. When the dog gets comfortable coming from a higher step, then move to the next step. Frequently, a dog will be able to move up the first three steps in a fairly short time (a few days) and then will not move when he gets to the fourth step. Just keep applying firm pressure on his leash and call him. He'll probably move down the next step and quickly go down the rest (he's mastered them). When he comes all the way down, praise him, "Good dog," and give him a food treat.

PHOBIAS OF OBJECTS

About three years ago, in the town of Brookline, Massachusetts, a wealthy suburb of Boston, I met Hannibal, a gigantic German shepherd. It was hard to imagine that this dog was afraid of anything; yet his owner, Dr. Brewer Nickerson, told me that whenever they went for walks Hannibal would pull him straight toward the bushes as soon as a car went by. Dr. Nickerson was a fairly big man, but even he was unable to restrain Hannibal once he became agitated.

I wasn't able to get any background information on Hannibal because, as Dr. Nickerson's wife, Betsey, explained, he just walked into their yard about three and a half months before. The Nickersons had made every effort to find Hannibal's owners, placing ads in the local newspapers and calling the area's animal centers, but they got no response.

After playing with Hannibal I could see that he had been well trained by his previous owner—he was excellent in all the basic commands. I asked Brewer to take Hannibal out for a walk so I could see how he heeled. The good doctor snapped out, "Hannibal, heel," and off they went, walking smartly down the street, with me trailing behind in my best Sherlock Holmes manner. Hannibal heeled very well by my exacting standards—until a BMW rolled down the street. Hannibal took one look at that four-door sedan and did his best Carl Lewis impression as he headed for a neighbor's meticulously kept hedges with Brewer in tow. When Hannibal dug himself a little hut, Brewer tried reaching in to pull him out, all the while saying, "It's okay, Hannibal," and patting him on the head. Finally, Hannibal calmed down and we resumed our little journey. The doctor, whose clothes were now thoroughly soaked with sweat and whose hands had been scratched in several places by the bushes, was exhibiting all the enthusiasm to continue on as a soldier on the Bataan death march. By this time I'd seen enough.

As the readers of this book should know by now, the good doctor was reinforcing Hannibal for the behavior he wanted stopped. What had to be done was to improve the dog's heeling just a bit and then when a car was approaching to say "Heel" and reward Hannibal through praise for doing the right behavior. It took a few days, but Hannibal was soon joining the national craze for walking.

Another object that scares dogs is vacuum cleaners. Frequently, somewhere in the past, someone may have pointed or even pretended to attack the dog with the cleaner's hose. Here's what I recommend. Leave the vacuum cleaner out so Bozo can become familiar with it when it's not on. Then I'd try staging a few, silent mock cleanings with it, again so the dog becomes used to seeing you use it. Don't try imitating the sound of a cleaner, as one Rich Little type of owner did; this just defeats the purpose of the procedure. Now put the dog in the room next to the one that you want to clean and command "Down" and then "Stay." Wait a few seconds and say "Good dog" and go quietly to the next room. If he stays down after you've flipped the switch on, great. If not, you have to go back and repeat the exercise. If he keeps breaking, then you should leave the vacuum on, and go back to the dog, commanding him "Down" and "Stay." Keep repeating until he gets it.

SPECIAL NOTE: PHOBIA OF GUNS

I'd just like to say a few words about phobias about guns since I'm sure some readers take their dogs hunting.

Here's what I suggest if your dog is afraid of guns. Purchase a cap pistol and take your dog out for a walk to a park. While you walk your dog at heel, have a friend approximately fifty yards away fire the cap gun once. Immediately give your dog a food treat, something he hardly ever gets—perhaps freeze-dried liver pieces. Timing is very important here. Don't wait to give the pup the treat. Immediately upon the gun shot feed the treat. Repeat this procedure daily if at all possible, with your friend progressively getting closer and closer. I cannot tell you when to have your friend get closer; you must be the judge of that. As long as your dog is accepting the treat and showing positive response, continue to have your friend get closer. Firing the cap gun during mealtime for the pup is also fine, but make certain you begin firing outside the house with the pup feeding inside the house. Distance is very important. And, of course, ignore neighbors and relatives who think you've gone crazy!

Provided your dog is doing well, progress to using a starter's pistol. Then seek out your local gun club, preferably a club that has trap or skeet shooting. Ask a member if it would be all right to bring your dog there. Begin by remaining a good distance away from the trap or skeet field—those guns are considerably louder than either gun you've used up to this point. While the guns are going off, play with the pup, making a game of it. Take your time in getting closer and closer. Remember, don't try to rush this program.

CHAPTER

9

Destructive Behavior

PHYLLIS Crenshaw, who cradled her six-month-old daughter, Susan, in her arms, was upset. "Mr. McSoley, this dog is like having another child."

Ms. Crenshaw and I were in her spacious kitchen on a bright January day. The sun beamed on her face, and although only in her late twenties, the strain of a new child and the behavior of her dog had taken their toll—she looked tired and wan.

Sitting near her feet, his large black and tan face scrunched up into quiet consternation, Moonie seemed by his mere presence to rebuke his owner's angry words. Moonie was a handsome dog, with the silky black coat and finely chiseled features characteristic of his breed, the Gordon setter.

Ms. Crenshaw had called me several days before complaining about Moonie's destructive behavior. He had been digging up her shrubs and clawing holes all over her backyard.

Shifting Susan to an upright position, Ms. Crenshaw continued. "Moonie is spiteful of Susan, I'm convinced of it. Every time I put him in the backyard he goes wild. I can't handle both of them. I quit my job as advertising executive to have a baby and all I do is try to keep the place from being destroyed by him," pointing her finger right at Moonie.

"Ms. Crenshaw," I said matter-of-factly, trying to diffuse the emotion of the moment, "Are you sure Moonie has only been acting like this since you had Susan?"

"Why, yes, I'm sure of it," she replied emphatically. "I remember very clearly that my husband, Morton, and I were down on the Cape until Labor Day and then we got back here on September third. That night I started to have labor pains. We went to the hospital and I came back a week later. I couldn't pay attention to both of them, so I put Moonie outside. That's when he started to go wild. He resents the attention we're paying Susan."

That didn't make sense to me. As a breed Gordon setters are known to be devoted family members, particularly good with children. I probed a little deeper.

"Ms. Crenshaw, tell me about your summer. How did Moonie behave down on the Cape?"

Ms. Crenshaw shifted Susan so she was propped up on her shoulder, and started to pat her back as she spoke. "Moonie was perfect all summer. He was out most of the day. My husband would take him on runs along the beach. And sometimes he would join some of my neighbors' dogs for runs."

She continued. "When he got back here, he started to run up and down the hallways a hundred miles an hour. We didn't have the time to take him for runs like in the summer and that's when we put him outside in the yard. We figured he could burn off his energy by himself. Instead he turned destructive."

We faced each other in silence for a moment as I turned over the facts in my mind. I looked down at Moonie, who still had not moved. I had seen it over and over again in my trips. Like humans who feel ill and go to a doctor's office and suddenly feel much better, dogs had the same capacity to never show me what their owners were describing.

I clapped my hands and called Moonie to my side. He jumped up and raced over, his eyes shining and alert, his long, elegantly pointed tail waving eagerly. "That's a good boy, Moonie," I said as I patted his luxurious fur. It was now time to solve this little mystery.

"Ms. Crenshaw, Moonie's destructive behavior has nothing to do with your daughter and he's not being destructive because he's spiteful—that's a human characteristic."

Ms. Crenshaw stared at me and was about to object when I interrupted. "What you did, unconsciously, during the summer was to condition a marathon dog."

"A what?" said Ms. Crenshaw.

"A marathon dog," I repeated. "By running all day, Moonie became used to six or seven hours of exercise. When you and your husband came home from the hospital and your attention was focused on Susan, you didn't bring Moonie out for his usual exercise. The week-long frustration caused him to start running indoors. When you put him outside he wanted to stay outside so he could run. He likes being outside, so every time you bring him in, he annoys you enough so he can go out again."

"But why is he tearing up my beautiful shrubs?"

"It's his energy level. Even though he's outside he's confined in the yard, so he's taking out his frustration by using his paws and mouth."

Ms. Crenshaw suddenly looked relieved. The secret guilt of not being able to care for both her child and dog was evaporating as she started to understand the true nature of the problem.

"What can we do to change Moonie?" she asked.

"There are several steps I want you to take. The first is you must get Moonie more exercise. I want you or your husband to take him out in the morning and the evening for at least half an hour. If you are taking the baby out for a walk, take Moonie."

She looked discouraged. "I can't do that. I can't push the carriage and walk with Moonie. He'll drag me down the street."

"Yes, you can," I assured her. "What you have to do is start teaching Moonie correct heeling, which we'll do along with sit, stay, and come when called. That will help you gain control of him. I also recommend that you determine when Moonie is going out. If he starts to make a fuss, have him lie down."

Within a couple of weeks, Phyllis called to tell me Moonie was behaving very well and she was looking forward to planting new flowers and shrubs in the spring.

The Crenshaw case is highly interesting because Moonie's destructive behavior could be interpreted as being caused by the baby's presence. But as you'll see more clearly when you read about introducing infants to dogs (Chapter Fourteen), Moonie's destructive actions had other origins. The clue was the summertime exercise, because destructive behavior is closely linked to the amount of exercise a dog gets, except this was a reversal of the usual pattern, when frustration and destruction occur from too little exercise.

The major causes of destructive behavior are boredom, frustration and separation anxiety. Lack of adequate exercise, improper chew objects (I only recommend a Nylabone or a Nylaring), lack of structuring, too much tug-of-war and other mouthy games, and emotional comings and goings lead the dog to take his frustration or boredom out in destructive behavior.

Here's a case where many of these factors were in play. Richard and Sarah Chin had an eleven-month-old cocker spaniel named Daphne who was destroying their cushions in their absence. They spoke to a trainer who told them when they arrived home to take a small section of the cushion and put it in the dog's mouth and tape it shut. The idea behind this was that Daphne would begin to hate the cushions.

What did the dog do? Upon their return she began to urinate in the living room. The trainer advised them "not to let her get away with that." The Chins now started to punish Daphne when they came home. The housesoiling didn't stop. After two weeks they visited a vet because they thought Daphne might have a urinary tract problem. That wasn't the case and the vet recommended me.

This is the program I set the Chins on, and owners with destructive dogs should follow it. Since the Chins worked at the same office they left for work together, intensifying the emotional impact of departure for Daphne. I told them to avoid emotional comings and goings, since that may heighten anxiety in the dog relative to being alone.

The Chins also had to engage in daily structuring before they left home in the morning, which would make Daphne feel more secure in her environment. They had to stop punishing the dog because she was urinating—all they were doing was conditioning an overly submissive dog—and never again tape her mouth shut. I told them to use a —Nylabone or a Nylaring as a chew object and I wanted to do the following exercise. I had them to place a cushion in the middle of the floor while they were sitting in the living room. If Daphne started toward the cushion, they should say, "No, bad dog." I asked them to put the pillow out once a night for two weeks.

I also made use of a chemical solution called Bitter Apple, which I sprayed on their couch. This solution has a taste that dogs don't like. I intensified Daphne's dislike by initially taking a Q-Tip, putting it in the bottle and dabbing a little on her tongue.

I had the Chins keep a chart of Daphne's destructive acts. And I warned them not to make a big deal out of them if she committed anymore. Just clean up the mess (not in Daphne's presence), and go about their business.

It took about six weeks but Daphne completely stopped attacking their cushions.

If this program doesn't work for you, then I'd advise crating. The cases in which I usually recommend crating right away is when the owner can no longer stand any destructive behavior, either because the dog has destroyed expensive property or because the owner has reached his or her breaking point.

SEPARATION ANXIETY

Most, but not all destructive behavior, takes place in the owner's absence. I remember a young female executive named Joan, lived in the Chestnut Hill section of Newton, Massachusetts. Her eighteen-month-old male Airedale named

Max destroyed a portion of her couch while she was sleeping in her bedroom one Saturday afternoon. (Max always slept on the bed with her. But this day she was so exhausted, she just wanted to sleep without her dog.) Why would her dog do such a thing? Acting out of spite would appear to be the logical answer. The dog, knowing her owner is in the bedroom, and finding the door closed, munches on the couch to express her dissatisfaction to the owner. Sounds like a good theory. But it is wrong.

What then is the reason behind this strange behavior? The answer is what clinical psychologists call separation anxiety. This means the owner's dog is so completely overdependent upon the owner for physical presence that the dog cannot control himself in the owner's absence. Hundreds of times I have been told by owners that if they so much as leave the room, Bozo follows them wherever they go. The dog becomes the owner's shadow. If the owner goes to the bathroom, the dog follows. If the bathroom door is closed, the dog may whine, scratch, or even attempt to chew the bathroom door, even though the owner is in there only for a few minutes.

How in the world does this happen? How do owners wind up with such neurotic pets? Incidentally, this is the only place in this book where you'll see the word "neurotic" used. I feel that dogs who suffer from separation anxiety are clearly neurotic creatures, and are truly hurting. (Usually it is a series of events that contributes to such a dog's condition.)

Let's look at a case that illustrates the behavior. Bob and Karen Kanter were a marvelous couple in their early forties. They lived in the city of Cambridge, located just across the Charles River from Boston. Their house, a few blocks from Harvard University, was situated on one of the tree-lined streets extending away from Harvard Square. The Kanters called me because their three-year-old mixed breed, Lois, was literally chewing her way through the house. Rugs, furniture, shoes, and other personal belongings were all fair game, as well as door moldings.

When I began to get a history of this cute little dog, Karen told me that her two children were both away at college, and with Bob working long hours (he was a physician in Boston), she suddenly found herself alone in their rather large home. So she decided to get a companion. The Massachusetts Society for the Prevention of Cruelty to Animals shelter in Boston had a puppy they estimated to be about nine weeks old, and when Karen saw that little ball of black fur, she knew it was the puppy for her. For a little over two years Karen and Lois were the best of friends. Lois was such a good puppy, extremely easy to housetrain, never much of a chewer, that Karen felt she had the perfect dog. She brought Lois everywhere: rides in the car, walks through Harvard Square, jogs along the Charles River. Lois was her constant companion. Then about four months ago, Karen told me, things changed dramatically.

"I would come home to find articles of my clothing pulled out of my closet. They wouldn't be destroyed, just dragged into the middle of the bedroom. After the first few episodes I became angry, and began to yell at Lois when I came home."

"Karen," I asked. "Home from where?"

"Oh," she said. "An old college roommate of mine called me several months ago and asked me if I would like to help her start a small catering company. Of course I was delighted, and we got together that very day. Since that time I have been spending several hours a day at Marianne's house, planning business strategy, all those things."

"And where was Lois?" I asked.

"Well," she replied, "I really couldn't take her with me to Marianne's house, so I had to leave her at home. It killed me to do so, but I really had no other choice. It seemed that things really began to get worse after I began to punish Lois for taking my clothes out of the closet. Mr. McSoley, I really think she resents my leaving her alone; she is slowly but surely destroying my house. Bob is beginning to get very angry as well, and I really can't blame him. It is so bad that now I bring Lois in the car to Marianne's, and leave her in there. She is fine in the car; however, the weather is getting warmer and there's really no shade where I park at Marianne's house. I'm afraid Lois will overheat. I'm really at my wit's end with this dog."

I looked at Karen. I looked at Lois, sitting on the couch next to Karen, snuggled up as close as she could possibly be to her owner. I asked Karen to walk into the kitchen and walk back. Karen got up, walked into the kitchen, followed by Lois close on her heels. Karen returned, and both Karen and Lois sat down on the couch again. "She always follows you around like that?" I asked.

"She is like a second skin," Karen answered. "Yet when I have a person come and sit for the dog, Lois is fine. She doesn't chew up a thing."

I then asked, "Karen, when you come home, before you were taking Lois with you in the car to Marianne's, did you give her a lot of attention?"

"Oh yes. I picked her up and hugged her, and Lois would run around, for about ten minutes after I got home. She is so cute and seems to love me very much. Why is she treating me this way?"

I replied, "Karen, Lois isn't remodeling the inside of your house because she is trying to get back at you. She is destructive because she is completely overdependent upon your presence in the house for her security. If you're not there, any person will be enough human presence to allow her to understand that she is not alone. However, when she's alone, she's unable to cope with it. Remember, for over two years this little dog spent all her time with you. You were never out of her sight. She was never alone. Your starting a new career has been a major crisis in Lois's life."

Karen looked anguished and said, "But Mr. McSoley, I really can't just pull out of the catering business, I'm committed to helping Marianne get it off the ground."

"I understand," I answered. "Let's see what we can work out."

What I did was set up the following program for Karen and Lois. We taught Lois the simple basic structures. I had Karen begin to tell Lois "Stay" several times a day when Karen left the room. At first Lois could not control herself, and would run after Karen. But Karen said nothing to Lois when she did that. She would simply return with Lois to the area where she was told to stay, and Karen would repeat the command. When Lois stayed, Karen would return and praise Lois—quietly. She removed all of Lois's old chew toys, and replaced them with a Nylaring for Lois. Karen and Lois played with the Nylaring a couple of times each day. Lois was no longer allowed on the bed at night, but was tied at the foot instead. Karen was told to begin to leave the house for short trips, under thirty minutes, when possible. I told her not to pat Lois before leaving, but rather to put Lois through a short, two-minute structure session. When she returned I told Karen to ignore Lois for several minutes until Lois calmed down, then to tell Lois "Sit," and when she did to give her some attention, but not a lot.

I told Karen to keep a daily chart on all destructive behavior done in her absence. Above all, I told Karen not to feel sorry for Lois, because, if she did, she would most assuredly begin to overindulge her again. I had Karen use Bitter Apple on previously chewed objects. The program took almost two months, but it worked. Karen and Marianne got their catering service off the ground, and Lois now tolerates being left alone.

One final note. Many puppies are brought up using rawhide chew objects. These objects intensify the dog's chewing, and he works on it until he gets it nice and soft, and then starts to pull and tear at it. This, of course, conditions the dog to pull and tear at other objects.

Some owners I've met give their dogs stuffed animals for play objects! Soon the dog rips at the cloth and starts to pull out the stuffing. From a Mickey Mouse doll to your couch is only a short step in the mind of your dog.

CHAPTER 10

Barking

"**M**R. McSOLEY, I insist. We're coming to the Ritz to have you work with Junior and Janey."

The voice on the other end of the phone was refined, civilized—but determined. Alfred Cook was a gentleman of the old school, but he knew how to get his way.

He had spent the last twenty minutes on the phone explaining his predicament. After living in Sugarhill, New Hampshire, all his life, he and his wife, both seventy-five years old, were moving to Florida in a month. But they had a problem—their pugs, Junior and Janey, were barkers. The lease at their new Florida condo specifically prohibited dogs with barking problems.

Mr. Cook implored me to come to Sugarhill for the month to work with the dogs. I said that was impossible because I couldn't neglect my other clients for such a long time. That's when he hit on the idea of coming to the Ritz.

"It's a fine solution," he said. "Mildred and I can go to the symphony and see Boston one last time before we leave. And," he laughed, "You can visit Junior and Janey every day for tea."

Three days later I found myself walking toward the

Ritz-Carlton Hotel, still a symbol of all that Boston represents—civility, sophistication, and a graceful way of life. It had been a number of years since I had last been to the hotel but little had changed. The gold handrails and marble floors still shone brightly. Slowly moving dowagers, down from Beacon Hill for lunch in the café, tapped along the lobby with their canes. Businessmen in gray suits clustered near the reception area, exchanging the latest economic news. Hotel personnel, in dark blue uniforms and white gloves, stood ready to attend to a guest's slightest need.

As I waited for the elevator I glanced at myself in its mirrored surface. A jacket and tie! Me. My clients would be amused that a man who invariably arrives in blue jeans and chamois shirts would be impersonating a junior executive. But the rules of the Ritz remain rigid—formality at all times. Standards are standards even for an animal behavioral therapist.

After a few seconds' ride on the elevator I found myself in front of the door to 309. I knocked and it swung open revealing, unmistakably, Mr. Cook. Tall and distinguished looking, he looked like Douglas Fairbanks, Jr., right down to the pencil-thin mustache.

Mr. Cook reached out, grabbed my hand enthusiastically and said, "Welcome, Mr. McSoley, welcome. So good to see you. Mildred, Mr. McSoley's here."

Mildred emerged from the bedroom with Junior and Janey in tow, who started barking furiously as soon as they spotted me. Almost as tall as her husband, she was a handsome woman, her long white hair demurely tucked in a bun, a style unchanged perhaps for sixty years. The two pugs barked away as she reached over to shake my hand and said, "Mr. McSoley, this is what we've had to put up with for years."

The Cooks told me that in the past they had tried the usual approaches to stop the barking—yelling at Junior and Janey; they tried muzzling them; and saying no whenever they would bark. Nothing worked.

Given the Cooks' age, the number of years the problem had persisted—Junior and Janey were seven—and the short time I had to work with them I decided to do a crash course of the McSoley Methods for Dealing with Barking. The first step was for the Cooks to attach a short line (approximately twelve inches) to Junior's and Janey's collars. Every time they barked I wanted the Cooks to say, "Junior, Janey, place." Then I asked them to go to the dogs, take them by the attached line to a predetermined spot—a corner in the hotel room—and command them "Down," then "Stay" for a minimum of two minutes. No matter how much barking they were doing, the Cooks should ignore Junior and Janey, and not say anything. When they had stopped barking for two full minutes, only then should the dogs be rewarded. I told the Cooks not to give any praise until after the two minutes, nor any after the release word. Praise them only for lying quietly in their place.

I informed the Cooks that I'd come by every other day and work with them on structuring the dogs until we got that under control. The final part of my plan to ensure that Junior and Janey would get enough chances to learn the correct behavior when someone came to the door. The Cooks requested Ritz personnel—room service, housekeeping, bell boys—to keep up a steady stream of knocking. Every couple of hours, someone should approach the Cooks' room. Long accustomed to meeting the unusual needs of the famous and the rich—one story has it that the Shah of Iran kept sheep in his room during a visit—the manager readily agreed to the plan.

Over the next three weeks, as is usually the case, Junior and Janey increased their barking! Why? Because they were receiving less attention than they usually got when they barked. They thus increased their barking, hoping to break down the Cooks' resistance. But as the Cooks followed the plan, Junior's and Janey's barking began to level off, then to fall. (I actually had the Cooks chart the number of times Junior and Janey barked so they could see the progress being made.)

On my last visit we put the dogs to the final test. Mr. Cook called down to room service, ordering champagne. We waited calmly for the next few minutes until there was a knock on the door. Mrs. Cook brought Junior and Janey to the corner of the room and said "Sit" and then "Down."

They obeyed immediately and didn't bark. Mr. Cook went to the door and opened it. The waiter—who looked as if this was not his first visit to the dog experiment room— wheeled in a tray with the champagne resting securely in a beautiful silver ice bucket. Junior and Janey eyed the waiter but remained quiet. Mr. Cook tipped the waiter, who then left. Still no sounds from Junior and Janey. Broad smiles broke across our faces. A resounding success! Mr. Cook reached over to shake my hand. "Wonderful. I never thought we could get this to happen."

"It just shows you," I replied facetiously, "what great hotel service can do."

Besides the techniques I employed, what the Cooks' story illustrates is that many owners live with a barking problem *for years* because they don't even hear the noise after a while, like people who live near subways. But when neighbors complain or owners have to move, they suddenly realize they have a barking problem.

The problem begins when the dog is young. Almost without fail, every client I visit with is pleased when that pup begins to bark, since it was viewed as part of the maturing process. These first barks may well sow the seeds for problem barking later on. Most owners praised their young dog for barking, telling him "Good dog" and giving him a pat or two. The praise was meant to reassure the pup that he's a good dog for alerting the owner to something. The pat was also intended to let the pup know that everything is all right and that he doesn't need to bark anymore. These good intentions aside, what this did was to sow the seeds for a barking problem.

The next stage went like this. Someone knocked at the door and the pup barked. The owner walked to the door, patted the dog, said "Good dog," and opened the door. The dog continued barking and the owner patted the dog again, saying, "Look Fido, it's Uncle Murray." The dog barked some more, but gradually calmed down in the presence of Uncle Murray.

Now every time someone came to the door Fido barked. Gradually the owner started to yell at the dog for barking. From Fido's point of view this was fine—everyone's barking. He's in charge of the door and he gets lots of attention whenever he barks. The dog is taking responsibility for the situation, not acting responsible to you.

Fido displayed what I call attention-demand barking. The owner has been reinforcing this behavior for a long time by all the attention he's given the dog. Sometimes, an owner provides even more reinforcement, although unknowingly, by giving his dog a food treat to calm him down. The owner finds himself in the kitchen when the dog starts barking and hands the dog whatever he is cooking while he goes to the door. This intermittent reward is the strongest conditioning tool the owner could use, except that he is unaware that he is doing so.

The program I put together for the Cooks is the best way I know to break a dog's habit of barking at the door whenever anyone comes calling. It requires patience and persistence. You must do it every time someone comes, weathering the inevitable escalation of barking at first. Gradually it'll subside and you'll gain control of the dog. Why does this approach work when the more conventional methods fail? Because this approach rewards the dog for doing the right thing, and the right thing is lying down. You may also approach your dog, tell him "Quiet" and follow with a blast on the horn. Bozo must be in his place when you do this.

Of course, another solution to barking is simply to let your dog know you're no longer going to tolerate this behavior. Go to your dog, say "Quiet," and immediately follow with an effective corrective shake. Stare at the dog, grab him on either side of the neck, say, "No," a quick shake and hold for twenty to thirty seconds. Keep holding eye contact. Then release slowly. This technique will only be effective, however, if you're already in a strong leader role with your dog. What will happen when the dog barks and an owner tells the dog to stop barking but he's not in a leader role? Not much. Here's a true story. Jeff Tudor and his wife, Eileen, lived on Cape Cod with their two-year-old Doberman, Toby, who would bark in an intimidating manner whenever anyone approached the house. A typical scenario went like this. The doorbell would ring. Toby would begin barking and running for the door, followed immediately by the Tudors leaping out of their chairs, yelling at Toby to be quiet and chasing him from the door.

When I arrived for my first visit, the Tudors repeated this act, with Eileen straddling the large Doberman with both feet firmly planted on the floor, her hands encircling a heavy chain-link choke collar. Within seconds Toby started to drag his petite blonde mistress toward me, all the while with Eileen yelling "Quiet." So don't try this technique unless you're already in control.

OUTDOOR BARKING

Outdoor barking is usually caused by the boredom and frustration the dog feels *just because he's outside*. I'm amazed owners don't understand this. Most owners who have this problem tell me that putting their dog outside is good for him. Owners think it's bad to coop up the dog inside. They can't be more wrong.

Several years ago a young woman named Judy hired me to help her with her fourteen-month-old German shepherd called Duchess. On the phone Judy told me that she had taken Duchess to a local obedience class, but the dog hadn't shown any signs of slowing down being a canine motor-mouth. Judy said, "The instructor told me I wasn't firm enough. 'You must get firmer, Judy,' this trainer kept telling me. I guess I just can't get firm enough, Ray." Of course, this had nothing to do with Duchess's problem.

That Duchess was way out of control was evident as soon as I rang the doorbell to Judy's ranchhouse. Duchess started barking immediately and I could hear Judy screaming behind the door. "Duchess, shut up, shut up right this minute, damn it!" Duchess kept right on going as I crossed the living room into the kitchen. As Judy and I talked through the onslaught of noise I realized what conversation must have been like during the London Blitz of World War II.

I asked Judy when Duchess did most of her barking, and Judy replied while she was away at work. Judy knew this because her neighbor was a nurse who worked the night shift and she could hear Duchess barking throughout the day. Judy said matter-of-factly, "I put Duchess outside in the yard just before I leave for work and she's basically outside until I get home around five. That is unless it's going to be a lousy day, then she stays in, because Duchess won't use the doghouse my husband built for her."

I questioned Judy further, asking why she kept Duchess outside. "Why, Ray, Duchess loves being outside in the sunshine."

I followed up. "Do you keep her outside in the winter months?"

"No, of course not, it's too cold."

"Then Duchess must be pretty bummed out around January and February."

"I don't think so, she seems to take it in stride. What are you getting at, Ray?"

"Well, Judy, I hate to tell you this, but you're completely off base about Duchess's thinking. She likes being inside and hates being outside. The reason she's barking is that *she doesn't handle being alone very well*."

Judy seemed completely surprised when I said this. I explained that Judy was isolating Duchess by putting her outside. I said, "For the first few minutes outside Duchess can check out the smells, eliminate, and run around. But after that there isn't anything for her to do until you come home. So she starts to bark to lessen her boredom."

What I told Judy to do to solve the barking was very simple—bring Duchess inside. It's like the old joke where a man goes to a doctor's office and says, "Doctor, my arm hurts when I wave it over my head." The doctor replies, "So don't do that." Judy followed my advice and Duchess has been a quiet dog ever since.

There are times when bringing the dog inside won't work—if the dog barks only when the owners are away. That was the problem Bill and Eleanor Hall had with their standard poodle, Butch, who was sixteen months when I met him. Butch was a smart, outgoing, willing-to-please dog except that he never stopped barking when the Halls left the house. I asked Bill and Eleanor to take a cassette recorder and record the dog's barking the next three times they departed. After they did this I returned to listen to the tapes and I could clearly hear that the dog was barking at something or someone. What it was I couldn't tell.

Since we couldn't remove the cause of the barking, I recommended that Bill and Eleanor buy the Tri-Tronics MBL Bark Limiter Collar. This collar is similar to Tri-Tronics' electric collar, except for some significant differences. For one thing the collar is completely self-contained—there is no separate transmitter controlled by the owner or trainer. Attached to the collar strap is a sensing unit, which is activated by the dog's throat vibrations when he barks. The instant Bozo barks, he hears a warning beep, and then receives a half-second low-level electric shock. The dog is not shocked every time he barks, but rather intermittently, which, as I explained previously, is the most powerful way to reinforce a behavior.

The collar worked wonders with Butch. Bill called me a week after they first tried the collar to report that Butch stopped barking almost immediately.

If you elect to teach your pet to control his barking with the collar, I'd suggest that you contact a professional familiar with its operation so that he or she may assist you getting off on the right foot with your dog.

CHAPTER
11

Disobedience

IN this chapter I want to talk about a set of problems that can be lumped under what I call disobedience. In each case—jumping up, dogfighting, unruliness when being groomed, and car problems—the owner can't control the dog. As a group, disobedience situations constitute a major headache for owners.

JUMPING UP

A while ago Bill Landen, a tall, white-haired man in his mid-fifties, asked me to see his golden retriever, Duffy, about his jumping up problem. As I entered the large colonial house in Grafton, Massachusetts, Duffy came flying out of nowhere, blindsiding me and knocking me back against the front door. In a reflex action, my left knee shot into Duffy's midsection, knocking him off me, but only momentarily. He launched his full eighty-six pounds of golden fur at me again. I tried two more quick knees, but without success. Duffy had me pinned against the door, hugging me for all he was worth, while Bill was yelling at him to get off and trying to pull him away. I told Bill that we should try to get to the kitchen. So Bill and I and Duffy moved slowly through the foyer, with Duffy playing a Ginger Rogers to my off-balanced Fred Astaire.

By the time we got to the kitchen, Duffy started to lose interest in his version of sumo wrestling and romped off to mangle a rawhide chew toy. As Bill poured me a Coke, he told me that Duffy had been acting like this for over two years. "I can't stand it anymore," he said, his voice shaking with emotion. "It's like getting mugged in your own hall-way every night. I'm afraid to bring guests home because of what Duffy will do to them." I asked Bill if he'd hit Duffy and he confessed that he'd belted Duffy on a number of occasions. "It seems to have no effect. I'm having fantasies at work of grabbing him by the throat until I choke the life out of him."

I'd seen this emotional state many times before—an owner pushed to the edge by his dog, unable to constrain himself from physically punishing the dog. Each repetition of the dog's behavior becomes like another drop in a Chinese water torture. What I had to do was break the vicious cycle that had become the only relationship between owner and dog.

Here's what I did. I asked Bill to give me a two-quart saucepan. Bill looked at me a little suspiciously but complied. I took the pan and filled it with enough water so that it would take about five or six minutes to boil. I then put a lid on it and turned the burner on high. In a short while the lid began to rattle. I then told Bill that this pan was going to help him train Duffy. Bill's expression had written on it, This guy must be nuts. But then I explained what I wanted him to do:

"When you come into the house at night to completely ignore Duffy's jumping up and proceed to the kitchen as best you can. Then fill the pot with water as I've done, cover it and turn the heat on high. Next, leave the room. Keep ignoring Duffy. Take your coat off, hang it in the closet, put your briefcase in your study. Return to the kitchen and stand by the stove until the lid begins to rattle. When it does, tell Duffy to sit. When he does, tell him he's a good dog and turn off the burner."

I added these final words: "I don't want you to yell at Duffy, hit him, or in any way provoke him. Just keep this up every day for three weeks and then call me."

I was sure when I left Bill that he thought I was an outpatient from a mental hospital. But there was much method to my madness.

Three weeks later Bill called and was very excited. "Ray," he exclaimed, "you're a genius. For the last few days when I walk through the door, Duffy runs to greet me, turns a couple of circles in front of me and then heads to the kitchen and sits by the stove."

What had happened? The little game I had Bill play had broken his anger and violent interaction with Duffy and had allowed the dog to calm down also. Rather than negatively reinforcing Duffy's jumping up, Bill wasn't reinforcing Duffy at all. Only when Duffy sat quietly did Bill give him attention.

What Bill never realized was his punishing the dog was a reward, as strange as it seems. He had conditioned a masochistic dog.

Here's another way to deal with jumping up behavior.

Marilyn Katz lived with her Boston terrier, Fred, who was one of the wildest jumpers I've ever met. Not only did this little dog jump nonstop when I crossed the Katzes' doorway, but he continued his routine all the way into the living room. As soon as I sat down, Fred launched himself into the air, landing in my lap.

"That's one of his favorite tricks," said Mrs. Katz dryly. "Members of my bridge club particularly like it."

"I'm sure they do," I replied, standing up to dump Fred on the floor.

As soon as I sat down, Fred flew right back into my lap. This time I dumped him harder. Fred didn't attempt another half-gainer. I turned to Mrs. Katz and said, "Tell your guests to do that to Fred every time he jumps on their lap." Then I asked if I could repeat my entrance to the house.

A couple of minutes later I rang the doorbell and was

greeted by Jumping Jack Flash. But this time the second
Fred began to jump on me, I said "Off" and my thumb hit
the button on the small boat horn I held behind my back.
BLAAAP. The sound of the horn shattered the quiet Katz
house. Fred leaped off my leg and fled from the room, racing
up the stairs to the safety of Mrs. Katz's bed. Before Marilyn
could speak I said, "Please, don't call your dog."

To my utter amazement, Marilyn went into hysterics,
doubling over in laughter for a good minute. When she re-
gained her composure, she dried her eyes and said, "That's
the funniest thing I've ever seen in my life. The little stinker
never jumped off anyone's leg before. Let's do it again."

I always like to see owners enthusiastically involved
in my experiments, so I told Marilyn to call a next-door
neighbor to repeat the procedure. She phoned Sue Wash-
burn, who in a short time rang the bell. Fred was still so
scared he didn't venture out until Sue had seated herself.
Fred did his high-flying act, landing on Sue's lap, but since
I already told her how to dump him she proceeded to plop
him on the rug. Fred scampered away again.

During the following week Marilyn used the horn three
more times when guests arrived. She also told her guests
to dump Fred when he jumped on them. Within two weeks
Fred's jumping up days were over.

You now have two ways of dealing with jumping up
behavior. In the first case we ignored the dog's unacceptable
behavior and provided him with what I call the positive
alternative—not getting attention until he sat. In Marilyn's
case I used a noxious negative stimulus, the boat horn. (For
more on how to use the horn see Chapter Six on object
guarding.) That coupled with the dumping cause the experience of jumping to become very unpleasant.

Try either method; both are highly effective.

Finally I'll give you three quick ways to stop Bozo from
banging into your chest or bothering guests.

My friends Don Wood, a Boston lawyer, and his lovely
wife Robin have an Irish setter named Webster who jumped
up on people. I suggested to Don and Robin that whenever
Webster jumped up on them simply to hold his front legs

firmly enough so he couldn't get down. Not squeezing the legs, just holding the dog in the jumping up position. When Webster got nervous and began to squirm and whine, I instructed Don and Robin to continue to hold. Only when Webster became truly panicky did I want them to let go, saying nothing and not looking at him.

This worked very well with Webster, who soon wanted nothing to do with this unpleasant experience.

A variation of this helps when dogs jump on kitchen counters. When your dog jumps up, quietly place the heel of your hand on Bozo's paw and push down—hard enough so that he wants to pull away and firm enough so that it's difficult for him to extricate himself. You may have to do this several times; many clients have had success with this technique.

If you have a dog that jumps at guests use this trick. Attach a screw eye hook to the baseboard of the room where you do most of your entertaining. When the guests are seated, bring Bozo in, tell him "Place" and hook him up on a short (approximately twenty-inch) line. Your guests and you should ignore his protests. Eventually he'll lie down and become quiet. He's now part of the party but not the star. In time Bozo will learn that his place is that particular area. Then all you have to do is to tell him "Place" and he will go there and not bother your guests at all.

DOGFIGHTING

Dogfighting can be a most serious behavioral problem, although the vast majority of dogfighting cases that I've had to deal with were more pushing and shoving incidents than serious bloodletting battles.

Margo Trustman lived just outside Los Angeles, California, with her husband, Jim, a Merchant Marine second mate. They also owned a cottage in the picturesque town of Camden, Maine. The Trustmans' three-year-old soft-coated wheaten terrier, Tug, attacked any dog that came near him.

She called me one day saying she was coming to Camden and wanted to pay me a visit to help her with her four-legged Genghis Khan. I agreed.

About a month after the call, Margo was sitting in my living room with her little hellion, giving me details of her past attempts to curb Tug's pugilistic propensities. A trainer in California who worked with Tug suggested he be put to sleep because he deemed him incorrigible. Tug was expelled from another obedience school for fighting. Margo had all but given up until she read the article about me.

I put down the coffee I'd been sipping during the briefing and told the attractive brunette sitting in front of me I had to see Tug in action. I called my next-door neighbor Holly Arnold and asked her if she would bring Cameo, her yellow Labrador, outside but to keep her on a leash. I then asked Margo to put Tug on his leash and we walked outside. Sure enough, as soon as Tug saw Cameo he immediately went into a frenzy, barking and snarling, standing up on his hind legs and pulling on his leash as hard as he could. Margo began yelling and hauling back on the leash, but it had no effect at all.

I took the leash from Margo, and for the next few minutes practiced heeling with Tug, both in my driveway and up and down the street. At first Tug was very unruly, continually turning toward Cameo. But after a few hard snaps and turns, Tug started to heel fairly well. I yelled over to Holly to bring Cameo down to the edge of her lawn, just near the sidewalk, and to keep Cameo by her side.

Tug and I walked past Cameo and Holly several times, initially twelve to fifteen feet away, then closing down to about six to seven. I then approached Holly and Cameo, getting within petting distance of that handsome yellow Lab. I told Tug to sit. Rather than sit, Tug suddenly lay down at the edge of the sidewalk. I began to pat Cameo and to talk to Holly in a very upbeat, friendly tone of voice. Cameo approached me and I began to pat both dogs, talking cheerfully with Holly, who was doing a splendid acting job. Then Tug made his move. He got up from the sidewalk, approached Cameo, and within a matter of seconds began to play with her.

I took the leash from Holly and brought both dogs back to my lawn, allowing them to play with each other for ten minutes. I glanced over to Margo, who looked as if she had just arrived at Lourdes. She just couldn't believe what she was seeing. Margo asked if I would come to Camden over a weekend to work some more on Tug.

That weekend I exposed Tug to eight dogs. Not only didn't Tug growl at any of them, he wanted to play with them all. On Sunday morning Margo, holding Tug on a leash, and I were standing on a grassy hill overlooking Camden harbor. About forty feet away was a large yellow Lab, standing near his owner, without a leash. Margo became quite anxious and asked, "Ray, what do you think will happen if that dog gets near Tug? I'm sure they'll fight."

I said, "They'll be fine." I then bent over and released Tug's leash. Margo stared in horror as Tug rocketed away toward Sunshine (we learned his name later when we talked with his owner). Sunshine spotted Tug and raced to meet him halfway. Both dogs started to romp and play. Margo kept looking at me as if I were Mandrake the Magician without a cape and top hat.

But I wasn't performing hocus-pocus. What I was doing was understanding how past training and Margo's behavior had conditioned her dog into fighting. You see, when Tug first went to obedience school, he was never allowed to interact with any of the other dogs. In fact, the trainer wanted all owners to discipline their dogs if they made any attempt to approach another dog in the training hall. Tug learned at an early age that not only were other dogs to be avoided, but that he would be punished whenever he got close to another dog. Margo, of course, reinforced Tug's anxiety around other dogs by her own anxiety.

I was able to get Tug to like Cameo for three reasons: my heeling exercise quickly established me as a firm and in-control leader; and my calm and happy attitude made being around me fun, and Tug's basic personality was not antagonistic toward dogs.

Of course, every dog who's a fighter doesn't respond as quickly as Tug. Some dogs are genetically predisposed to be aggressive toward other dogs, born, so to speak, with little zip guns in their paws. But don't immediately put your dog in this Rebel Without a Cause slot. Go to a qualified professional trainer for advice about your dog and work with him on heeling and creating a happy environment when you bring Bozo near another dog.

UNRULINESS WHILE GROOMING

This ranges from simple problems of the dog not standing still to Bozo nipping at the brush to his biting your hand.

Here's what to do when you have these problems. If you basically have good control over the pup, but he becomes a bit unruly, squirming around or biting the brush, either one of two approaches will usually work. First, hold the pup with one hand by the collar and begin brushing with the other. The minute he begins to misbehave tell him

Proper grooming. It feels great!

"No" and immediately follow the "No" with two or three firm shakes, or holding on both sides of his neck, having him face you, holding eye contact for 30–40 seconds before releasing. If Bozo remains calm, quietly praise him. If he acts up, shake and bake.

If this doesn't work, an alternative involves using food as an incentive. While the dog is standing or sitting, begin brushing. A friend or relative should be nearby holding some food treats. If the dog behaves, give him a food treat. Be selective with the treats. What you want is to have the pup focus on the treat rather than the brushing, and to associate brushing with good things.

Of course, another approach is simply to bring the dog to a good groomer. Good groomers are excellent dog handlers and you can learn a lot if you work with one that can control your dog. The groomer will charge you for the lesson but the money will be well spent.

CAR PROBLEMS

On a couple of occasions as Mary and I were driving back from Cape Cod we got behind a maroon Oldsmobile inhabited by a middle-aged couple and two West Highland white terriers who sat in the back. Whenever a car passed the Olds the two terriers would go crazy, barking furiously and bouncing around the back of the car like members of a circus tumbling team. I remember wondering how that couple could stand the noise; with the windows closed because of air-conditioning, that car must have sounded like being trapped inside Big Ben at noon.

But hundreds of my clients have lived with such behavior for years before I visited with them. Howard and Betty Sills, for example, have a large Great Dane named Bentley who liked to go nuts whenever they drove into gas stations. As they pulled near the pumps, Bentley would begin to bark. When the attendant approached the car, Bentley would start to growl. And when the poor man began to fill the tank, Bentley would smash into the rear window, barking and snapping.

Paying for gas was even more hazardous. As Howard tried to restrain Bentley, Betty would squeeze out of the car, close the door quickly and conduct the transaction outdoors. This plan worked for several months until one late afternoon when the Sillses rolled into their station for gas. While the attendant began pouring the gas, Bentley started to claw frantically at the window, which quickly turned into a savage attack on the leather upholstery. Betty, hearing the sound of tearing leather, yelled at Howard to stop Bentley. Howard, in turn, hollered at Bentley and tried to grab him by the collar. Bentley would have none of that and promptly bit down hard on Howard's hand and continued methodically to shred the back of the car until they pulled away.

I began to work with Bentley the next day, immediately trying to improve his heeling, which wasn't good. I also worked on his down command, which he had learned in obedience school, but which was never reinforced thereafter. I had the Sillses have Bentley lie down for up to one hour during the evening while they were either reading or watching television. And I had them put Bentley in the down position when they were walking him and saw another dog.

All of this was done over a three-week period. During this time I had them refrain from going to the gas station with Bentley. But in the fourth week of the program I told them it was time to put Bentley back in the car; me and Betty in front, Bentley by himself in back. Howard stayed home. As we drove toward the station, and we saw a dog, I made certain that Bentley saw his canine brother and immediately told him "Down." I kept him in this position for two minutes. At the end of the ride I told Betty to do this daily and said I'd see them next week.

The following week I announced that we were going back to the station. Betty told me that the owner of the gas station had informed her that Bentley was no longer wanted at his station. I said, with all the confidence I could muster, that there wasn't anything to worry about.

The only way to travel, relaxed and calm.

The proper crate for Bozo.

As we pulled into the station, with Betty mumbling about what a fool idea this was, I told Bentley "Down" and "Stay." Bentley grudgingly went into the down position. A young attendant approached, Betty lowered her window about two inches and asked him to fill the tank. As the gas was being pumped, the attendant started to clean the front window. I leaned over to Betty and said, "Ask him to do the rear window." What little blood was left in Betty's face drained away as I finished my sentence.

Betty lowered her window again and made her request. The attendant retreated to the back of the car as Bentley followed his every step. I repeated "Stay" and Bentley didn't move, or even growl. Betty lowered her window again and handed the young man some cash. He went back to get change and a few minutes later emerged with the station manager, who came over to the car. He stared into the backseat where Bentley and I were calmly sitting and said, "Glad to see you got yourself a new dog, Mrs. Sills. That old one was a terror."

The key to car problems is to follow the procedure I used with Bentley. You must remain in control when you're in the car and this can only happen if you have control *before* you enter the automobile.

SECTION

III

CHAPTER

12

Puppies

I BELIEVE many dog problems can be prevented if owners think about why they are buying a dog, if they have some guidelines for buying a puppy, and if they engage in basic structuring during the pup's first six months.

Unfortunately, many owners don't think about or know what they're doing. When I ask owners what they thought about before they bought their dog they look at me blankly and say, "Well ... uh ... we went into the pet store and looked over some dogs. Daisy was so cute that we bought her for our daughter." Amazing. A decision involving a ten-to-fifteen-year responsibility given so little consideration. And when I ask what kind of structuring activities they conducted during the pup's first months, many owners believe a dog is too young for such discipline. Such ignorance leads to trouble.

Many owners who buy puppies simply have not thought out what they're looking for in a dog, what kind of breeds are capable of fitting into their life-style, what pup within a litter is most likely to be compatible with them, and what kind of environment is best for a puppy. Although these are commonsense questions, few dog owners ever ask them. The result is many unhappy dogs and owners.

In this chapter I'm not going to discuss all aspects of puppy care—that's another book. Rather I want to leave with you three concepts: how to think about buying a puppy; how to test for a puppy that's right for you; and what you should do to bring up a puppy during the first six months, the most crucial period of time in the owner-dog relationship. When I'm through you should be well equipped to select and bring up your next pup.

PICKING A PUPPY

I have conducted many puppy seminars and I always discuss how to buy a puppy. I always begin my lecture by telling the audience that the first thing they should think about before buying a puppy is their life-style and their emotional needs. These are the kinds of questions you have to ask yourself: Are you a busy professional couple with two small children living in the city with little spare time? Then don't get a dog that has a high energy level and requires large amounts of exercise. Are you a person with an aggressive personality? Then stay away from a dominant-tempered puppy—you may wind up killing each other as he matures. Is your family ready for the responsibility of a dog? Are you? Generally speaking, more than one family member should be involved in caring for the dog, but leadership can't automatically be transferred; it has to be earned. If you're not sure why you're getting a dog, then keep asking yourself these kinds of questions.

There are endless variations on the personalities of owners and their life-styles. Ponder your own situation *before* you start thinking about what kind of dog you want or you'll be taking the first steps toward creating a serious dog problem.

Next, find out what breeds have characteristics that most fit your life-style and personality. I recommend you read Dr. Daniel F. Tortora's *The Right Dog for You* (Simon and Schuster, 1980). This is an invaluable guide that provides simply written and highly informative descriptions of each dog breed. Thumb through the book and pick out three to five breeds that you like.

After you've done this, attend a dog show. Don't be intimidated, you'll have a lot of fun. At the show, question breeders about the dogs you've tentatively selected. Size up the breeders. Ask them about the particular dogs you're interested in, but be considerate of their time during the show. If one seems particularly frank and knowledgeable set up an appointment.

Why am I recommending breeders? Since they only handle one type of dog they're more likely to give you a more honest and intelligent answer than pet shop owners. Most breeders love the dogs they're raising and want their puppies to have a good home. Breeders often refuse to sell puppies to certain people because they feel the potential owners are not a good match for the dog.

What's wrong with pet shops? They handle several dozen breeds—cutting down their knowledge about any particular one—and these stores frequently obtain dogs from "puppy mills," farms that raise dogs on demand, which give little thought to a sound breeding program or a proper environment. Many times, these mills remove puppies from their mothers and litter mates at an early age to meet pet shop requests for dogs. This can cause severe behavioral problems, as I'll discuss later in this chapter. A final problem with these stores is that puppies live in a bad environment—before they're bought, they've often been exposed to and handled improperly by too many people. You may get a good dog from a pet shop; but more likely you're asking for problems.

There are, of course, bad breeders. I know of no way to guarantee that you will get a good breeder. Buying a pup is like any other consumer transaction—go into it with your eyes open. You have to be informed and you need to take your time. Don't bring a checkbook with you the first time you go. Don't be rushed into making a choice if you're not sure. Spend time with the breeder. Find out about the dog's pedigree, but don't be snowed by it. All a pedigree tells you is about that dog's family tree. It doesn't insure that *your* dog will be nice or even-tempered. A pedigree will, however, tell you a lot if you are familiar with some of the names in it.

A final bit of advice. If you're through talking with a breeder and you have doubts, walk away. There are plenty of other dogs and other breeders.

You should talk with at least two or three breeders before you make any choices. This expands your understanding of the breed you're interested in obtaining. You'll also be gaining experience evaluating how breeders respond to your questions, thus making your eventual selection easier.

If a breeder tells you that a breed's not for you, don't get angry. He or she has given you valuable information. Maybe your assessment of your personality and life-style wasn't objective enough? Or maybe you've misunderstood the breed's characteristics? If a breeder rejects you, stop and think.

Once you've a comfortable relationship with a breeder, spend some time with him looking at his puppies. The breeder should provide you with insights into the puppy's behavior.

After your visit with the breeder it's a good idea to contact your local veterinarian and discuss possible congenital and genetic problems associated with the breed—such as hip and eye problems.

TEMPERAMENT TESTING

For a number of years I've been temperament testing puppies. These tests were designed by William Campbell, who described them in *Behavior Problems in Dogs* (American Veterinary Publications, 1975). Campbell's tests only indicate the direction a puppy may take. How you treat and train has much to do with his behavior. But if a pup tends toward any of the extremes the tests pick up, then you may want to pick another puppy.

Campbell's tests help determine whether the dog is overly dominant or overly submissive, independent or in the middle. Based on my use of the tests, I've added two more categories—the shy pup and the cautious pup. The puppy you pick should be in the middle—a mildly submissive dog. However, I must add that just because a dog tests overly dominant, overly submissive, independent, shy, or cautious doesn't mean he won't be a good dog. I feel that dogs with these behavioral tendencies should be bought by experienced dog owners. If this is your first time, stick with a mildly submissive dog.

Here's how to conduct temperament testing. Only one person should perform these tests and you should test each pup that you're interested in separately. Use an area unfamiliar to the pup—a corner of the breeder's yard might be ideal. You should be the major attraction during the test. Avoid being near distractions in the background, such as loud music or lawn mowers. And always ask the breeder to watch you do the tests—he or she is probably familiar with them and can help you make your pick. But make sure the breeder is out of the puppy's sight, since his or her presence will influence the test.

There are five tests in this procedure.

Test One

Put the puppy down and walk away from him. Clap your hands, squat down, and call him in a loud, cheerful voice, "Here, here."

If the pup bounds over, jumps up on you, and is overly friendly, this is a sign of a dominant pup.

If Bozo doesn't come over at all, then he's displaying independence.

If the pup comes over, falls to the ground and rolls over on his back, then he's showing overly submissive behavior.

If the pup comes over in a friendly but not overbearing manner, his tail wagging and a glad-to-see you expression on his face, he's showing mildly submissive behavior.

If the pooch keeps staring at you and doesn't come at all, he's being shy.

If the pup stares at you but comes over hesitantly, he's being cautious.

Walk away and clap your hands . . .

. . . squat down and call "Here, here."

What you're looking for is the mildly submissive pup. But don't downgrade the pup who takes his time to approach, and then gets friendly—he can be a great puppy. You'll have to wait to make a judgment on him until you get the rest of the scores.

Test Two

This is a simple test—just place the puppy on the ground and walk away.

If the pup follows you, then he's displaying submissive behavior. Give him a gold star because that's what you want.

If the pup runs in front of you, jumps all over you and nips at your pants—watch out. He's exhibiting dominant behavior. No star for him.

And if Bozo runs off to sniff the flowers? Then he's an independent type who may keep thumbing his paw at you in later years.

In this test the shy dog will probably just stare and not follow, while the cautious dog probably will follow since he has gained a familiarity with you.

A warning. Many people find overly submissive behavior affecting. They see the pup as needing their love. Be careful—you may have a dog with such problems as being timid with people and you'll wind up being a "canine social worker."

Test Three

This is another easy test for independence, because you have a lot of interaction with the dog.

Crouch down and pat the pup. Is the pup content while being petted? An aggressive pup will jump at you or try to take a nip out of your hand. An independent dog will walk

Just walk away from pup.

away; an overly submissive one will roll over on his back; the shy one will back away; and the cautious dog will let you pet him. The gold star pup is a submissive one, who enjoys the petting, and wags his tail eagerly.

Test Four

This test is for dominance and is a little more complicated. Place the pup on his back by turning him over on the ground and putting your hand on his stomach. Hold for sixty seconds. Don't remove your hand for any reason, even if the pup yelps, vocalizes, or tries to bite your hand. Gradually the pup should calm down. If he puts up no resistance he's showing submissive behavior. If the puppy continues to bite and vocalize throughout he has overly dominant characteristics. (This test doesn't show shy, cautious, or independent behavior.)

Test Five

This is the last test. Take the puppy around his middle with both hands and lift him slightly off the ground for thirty seconds. Like test four, this exercise indicates the dog's level of dominance. If the dog frantically flails his legs, he's showing dominant behavior. If he lies quietly, he's being submissive. The pup who wriggles initially, but who then tolerates being held is behaving fine. (This test doesn't detail shy, cautious, or independent behavior.)

What have these tests shown? They indicate each pup's *tendency* toward his particular temperament. My suggestion is to pick a puppy in the middle range, with a mildly submissive temperament. He'll be eager to follow your lead as he matures, yet still have enough spirit to give you years of mutual love and enjoyment.

Crouch down and pat the pup.

What do you do if one has inconsistent scores, or who appears to mess up one test? Repeat the test immediately and rescore the pup.

Finally, always ask the breeder how he or she scored the dog. See how your tests compare. Listen carefully to the breeder's opinion. Although I've found temperament testing to be a useful tool, I still believe a *good* breeder is your best judge of the pup.

PUPPIES—THE FIRST SIX MONTHS

The first six months of a dog's life are crucial. Many owners have little idea of a pup's stages of growth or what they

Place the puppy on his back and put your hand on his stomach.

should be doing to establish the proper relationship with their pup. Without such knowledge and understanding, the odds of having a happy and well-behaved dog are low. At a much earlier age than most owners suspect, a pup is capable of some conditioned learning. Behavioral scientists now believe that a pup can begin as early as five to seven weeks.

There are five developmental periods in the first twelve weeks of a pup's life:

- Neonatal
- Transitional
- Early socialization
- Peak imprinting
- Final socialization

Take the puppy, lift slightly off the ground and hold for thirty seconds.

Neonatal: From Birth to Day Twenty

Roughly speaking, this period covers the first twenty days of a pup's life. He basically eats, sleeps, and eliminates. He also undergoes considerable physical development. The pup needs his mother the most during this critical period. The pup is aware only of heat, cold, and pain. He can't be taught anything during this time. Around fourteen days the pup's eyes open.

Transitional: Weeks Two to Four

This period lasts from the end of the second week through the fourth week. The pup still needs his mother a great deal, but he's now capable of simple learned behavior. He begins to look more like a puppy and starts to play with his litter mates, biting and chewing on them. Permanent removal from his mother and litter mates during this week can cause drastic emotional problems, such as the dog being unfriendly toward other dogs. The shift from neonatal to transitional, however, occurs almost immediately. It's like an electrician wiring a house for twenty days. On the twenty-first day he throws the switch and all the electrical components in the house operate. The same is true of pups— suddenly they're capable of learning.

Early Socialization: From Day Twenty-Nine to Forty-Nine

From twenty-nine to forty-nine days is a critical phase in the pup's life. He's maturing rapidly now. During these weeks, puppies should begin receiving increasing amounts of human contact, a little at first, then more and more. (Scientific tests have shown that puppies who receive *no* human contact up to thirteen weeks become catatonic near humans when they're later exposed to them.) This is why it's ideal for a puppy to move away from his litter mates and his mother between seven and eight weeks and move in with his new owners. That's his *peak* period of socialization.

By the time puppies are seven weeks old, the pecking order within the litter has been established—the boss has emerged, as well as the runt. The other puppies have structured themselves within the canine hierarchy. This is the other reason for removing the pup around seven or eight weeks. The longer the puppies remain together, the more permanently ingrained the canine pecking order becomes. After eight weeks it may become increasingly more difficult to break that imprinting.

Peak Imprinting: Weeks Eight to Ten

This is when the pup's character can be molded the most easily. The pup is also most susceptible to being frightened by sudden, loud sounds and movement. If a pup receives a severe fright he may carry the fear all his life. This period is the time when the pup normally makes his adjustment to moving in with a family. Basic structuring should be started during this period.

Final Socialization: Weeks Ten to Twelve

At the end of this time, the pup should have adapted nicely to his new home. If he has had good, positive human contact from five weeks through twelve, then the essential basis for a healthy relationship should be established.

And it's because of this that I don't recommend that owners buy a puppy if he's over thirteen weeks. A great opportunity has been lost to develop the proper bonding between pet and owner.

BRINGING UP A PUPPY

Remember my first rule about the need for proper communication with your dog. Communication begins from the moment you pick up your pup. And like the other areas I've discussed, I have definite ideas about what you should be doing to achieve good communication.

You and Your Puppy's First Day

You may not realize it, but there's a preferred day to pick up your new pooch—Friday. This gives you the weekend to devote attention to the pup's needs and is usually the most relaxed time during the week.

I suggest you ask your breeder to let your pup wear a simple buckle collar for a few minutes a day for a couple of days before you pick him up. This cuts down the number of new things the pup has to be introduced to when he makes the trip home.

You should call the breeder before you pick up your pup to find out what kind of food he or she has been feeding the dog and continue using that brand. You should also get the pup's feeding schedule so you can follow it.

Before leaving the breeder you should have the pup eliminate prior to making the ride home, particularly if it's a long trip. (If your pup is being flown to you, wait until after the tenth week, so that the puppy is through his fear-imprint period.)

Once in the car, place your pup on the seat next to you. This is his first time away from the breeder and he may be anxious. As you drive, keep one hand on him and periodically talk to him in a quiet voice. Don't pick him up while driving. And don't let other family members prod or poke him. Let him relax. If he falls asleep, that's ideal.

Housetraining also begins on this day. *Before* you enter your house take your pup to the spot outside where you want him to eliminate. If he goes right away, say to him *as he is going* "Hurry up" five or six times, then tell him "Good dog" immediately after he's finished. Pet him once or twice, then bring him into your house. If he doesn't go right away, play with him for a few minutes, not roughly, and when he goes, repeat the above procedure.

Now bring him inside but don't make a big production out of it. Just walk in and introduce him to other members of the family. After they've pet the pup for a minute or two, have them resume their normal activities. Also make sure the neighbors and all your children's friends don't storm the house looking to pet the dog. He needs quiet.

Introduce your pup to the house that day. The best way to do this is to put him on a collar and leash and bring him with you to a room. Sit in a chair with the puppy on the floor next to you and read a paper or a book for a few minutes. Take him off the leash and let him scamper around, exploring the new sights and smells, but keep him in sight. Then move to another room. When you've finished this tour, bring your puppy to where he is going to sleep that day—preferably a corner or under a table. When he looks like he's ready to snooze, bring him to that spot. Or you might let him select his own spot. I've done that with my own puppies and it's always worked out well.

When he wakes up take him outside immediately. Repeat what you said early—"Hurry up" (five to six times) while he's going, followed by "Good dog" as soon as he's finished. Then bring him back inside. Remember, there are three times when you must take out the pup—when he wakes up, shortly after he eats, and after he has run around inside (this is when the pup's energy is so great that it looks as if he's having a fit).

Now comes the time to pick an area for the pup to sleep. My suggestion is that you have the pup sleep in your bedroom for the night in a dog crate. I want him sleeping near you. The crate should be the proper size for your puppy. Your breeder can advise you what brand and what size crate to purchase.

When you're ready to retire, simply put the pup in the crate, close the gate, turn out the lights, get into bed and *ignore* the pup's whining. If you do anything to calm the puppy you'll be reinforcing that behavior. After a while, your pooch will understand that whining won't get him anywhere and he'll nod off to sleep.

The importance of crating should be clearly understood. If your pup is introduced to it properly and at an early age, he'll adapt to it nicely. Not only can the crate be used at night, but it can be used during the day for *short periods* during his sleep periods. It can also be used for a short time if you and the pup want a break from each other. The value of crating also comes into play when your dog is an adult and must be kept quiet at home, during illness or after an operation. Crating is not a good idea for long periods of time, however, since it can contribute to hyperactivity, because the dog has no way to release his energy.

Now be prepared to get up every two hours to take the dog outside. I know this isn't easy. I didn't like doing this with my dog Jake. I got a few icy stares from Mary when I stumbled out three times during the first night to take Jake outside. But this will be over in two or three days and your pup will be well on his way to being housetrained. I promise. By the second week, I could get up at 5:30 to 6:00 and take Jake out. If you can get your partner to take a shift do so.

But for this first day you have to adjust your life. Just take a patience pill and realize you just started a wonderful new relationship.

The First Twelve Weeks

Here are the activities I want you doing the first couple of weeks with your puppy.

Housetraining
I won't go into specifics on housetraining, since it is covered in detail in Chapter Seven. However, unless it's absolutely necessary I suggest you don't papertrain your dog. It teaches your dog that it's acceptable to eliminate inside the house. Later on, you'll have a more difficult time *retraining* him to go outside.

Proper diet and a daily schedule help housetrain your pup. Feed him either three or four times daily, using a good puppy chow (the one from the breeder is fine).

Structure

It's important to start putting a little structure into your dog's life and it can be executed around the kitchen table while you're eating your Cheerios!

Here's how it's done. Go to your local hardware store and get two snaps, similar to those on the end of a leash, and a screw eye hook. Make up a short line (rope or nylon), around sixteen inches. Screw the eye hook into the baseboard in your kitchen and attach one end of the line to it. When it's time for you to eat, quietly take him by his buckle collar, tell him "Place," lead him to the area you've selected (select an area large enough so he'll be comfortable when he's a full-grown dog), and hook him to the line. Eat your dinner, ignoring his protests. Don't even look at him. After he's stopped vocalizing and is lying quietly, look over and tell him quietly "Good dog." From now on that's his place during meals. Screw eyes can also be placed in the den and the living room. Teach your pup to "Place" there as well. Later, when he's grown and you are entertaining in the living room, simply tell your dog, "Place," and he will without being hooked.

Chew Objects

You should also be introducing pup to his first chew objects. As I said before, the only objects I recommend are Nylabone or a Nylaring. Both are very hard plastic-type chew objects which are harmless to your puppy but provide him with necessary chewing.

Correction

When to begin correcting the puppy? I suggest you don't correct during his first week with you. This is a time of adaption; correction, if not executed properly, can have long-term negative effects, setting the tone for the rest of the relationship. Instead of "No," teach him to sit that first week. The first lesson your pup should learn from you is something positive: "When I do the right thing I get praised," your pup will think.

But by week two you should start to correct for mouthiness—biting your hands when you're petting him. This is normal canine behavior, although some puppies bite more, some bite harder. Mouthiness has to be discouraged—unchecked, your beloved pup will start chomping down on assorted relatives and friends.

Stopping the pup from biting is your first battle of nerves. In my experience, owners usually lose this fight, winding up undercorrecting, which is virtually useless. Here's the way I did it with Jake. I laid him on his right side on a carpet. I was on my knees with Jake's head a few inches in front of my right knee. I placed my right hand at the back (scruff) of his neck, not grabbing, just laying it there. With my left hand I began to pat him, working my way up to his muzzle. When Jake began to bite, I told him firmly "No," and followed it with a shake of the neck, which I was still holding by the scruff. I shook him several more times, still holding his scruff, until Jake released his grip on my fingers. When Jake let go, I slowly released the scruff of his neck, taking maybe two or three seconds. Then I began patting him again after a pause of perhaps ten seconds. Jake bit again, and I repeated the procedure.

If your pup yelps during the correction, that's all right; he'll stop soon. He's only in minor distress. After a few corrections, your pup will understand that when he hears the cue word "No" and if he stops what he's doing, he can avoid shaking. After a while you'll no longer have to shake.

Jake learned after two repetitions. Some pups take longer. Jake, you must understand, had been taught how to sit, and was lying in place during meals, so he already had learned some control.

On this exercise, don't pull your left hand away from the pup's mouth and then attempt to correct. If you do, you're not correcting him for biting, but for releasing, since the correction occurred after the release. Also, remember to tell your pup "Good dog" when he's lying quietly accepting your petting without biting. *Keep correction to a minimum.* You should gain leadership with your puppy through positive reinforcement and simple structuring.

Exercise

It's important that your pup get proper exercise. A couple of romps on Saturday and Sunday, sandwiched in between trips to the beach and the supermarket won't do. Daily exercise—two (or more) short sessions—is part of pet ownership.

Your pup will go through a streak of frenzied activity, followed by immediate sleep. He'll also have what earlier I described as fits, which are most likely to occur between 5:00 P.M. and 8:00 P.M. When they come, take him outside—it's only pent-up energy and it has to be released. And please, *no roughhousing* and *no tug-of-war.* Those games involve socially dominant behavior and can condition aggressive behavior.

So how should you have fun with Bozo? Talk to him and pet him, work on the basic commands, play retrieve. Not all pups retrieve, but most will, particularly if you begin early enough. I began tossing a new paint roller for Jake when he was nine weeks old. I did it every morning around 5:30 in the basement. Give your dog lots of praise when he brings back your version of the paint roller. And stop the game before he gets tired of it, so that he wants one more toss. That's the way you build enthusiasm for the game.

As the weeks go by, your pup will have greater control over his bladder and therefore you should adjust his going-out schedule based on this fact. You should change your own schedule as well. You should leave him for your various activities without feeling sorry or guilty. Please don't make a big deal out of your comings and goings. It just builds up anxiety, and may, down the line, lead to destructive behavior. In fact, I'd ignore Jake when I returned, except for a "Hi, Jake." I never wanted Jake to think he's the main reason for my coming back to the house.

When you enter your house, you should greet everyone else, and then acknowledge your pup. As soon as he learns to sit, have him sit before you pat him. In that way you prevent him from learning to jump up. That's why Jake doesn't jump on people. When he sat he got attention; when he jumped I completely ignored him.

By the time your pup is thirteen to fourteen weeks old, he should be going for daily walks, seeing and experiencing the world. When you meet people have him sit. And—I know this is hard—ask people not to make a big deal about Bozo, just a pat or two and a "Good dog." Again, you don't want to teach him that he's the center of attention.

As you and pup progress toward the sixteenth week, you should be teaching structuring (see Chapter Three on structure), working on housetraining, and extending the limits you've established, such as having pup lie down quietly next to you while you're reading. A good way to accomplish this is by using the screw eye hook and lead that worked so well in the kitchen. Put one hook in your den, another in your living room. Tie him to the hook and repeat the procedure I described for the kitchen. Wherever *you* put the hooks become his places. As he matures and you're entertaining in the living room, you simply tell the pup "Place" and he'll go to that spot and lie down.

The period between the day you first bring your puppy home and four months is highly critical. During this time you should accomplish the following:

- Housetraining—Bozo should be well on his way to minding his manners by going outside.
- Structure—Your pup should know how to sit, stay, lie down, heel, and come when called. He won't be perfect, but he's getting there.
- Limits—The puppy should understand the cue word "No."
- Play—He should be chewing on his Nylabone or Nylaring and retrieving.
- Integration—Your best friend should now be part of the family, familiar with the entire house, and a gentleman during meal times, lying quietly while the family eats.
- Exercise—He should be going out for short walks.
- Healthy relationship—Your pup and you should be having a great time, with both parties happy with each other.

Teaching sit properly to a puppy. Begin with a treat...

get up on your legs, still bent over...

and pup goes into sit naturally.

If this sounds mind-boggling, relax. If you're behind, just keep plugging. This is a time for you and your dog to get to know each other, to have fun together, and to make allowances for each other's mistakes.

FOUR TO SIX MONTHS

The four-to-six-month stage in a pup's life is a transition, a kind of preadolescence. You'll see a dramatic change in your pup. Many pups who are outgoing prior to this time now become very shy. Don't panic. In two to three weeks it'll pass and your puppy will be fine. Don't punish Bozo for this behavior, because it'll be counterproductive. Ride it through by continuing to structure the pup.

Your major concern through the four-to-six-month period is to earn your leadership over the pup. You should be incorporating structuring into your daily activities with your pup in a variety of ways.

Here's how I was working with Jake when he was five months old. I was building structure in very small doses through such simple activities as going out the door, getting in the car, getting out of the car, and exercising.

I began this way. Standing in the kitchen I'd call, "Jake, come." When he arrived I'd tell him to sit and I'd put on his leash. We'd walk to the door together, and then I'd tell him "Sit" and then "Wait." I'd open the door and walk outside. I'd tell him "Okay" and then he'd come through the door.

When we'd walk over to my station wagon I'd tell Jake to sit and I'd open the tailgate. Jake would wait until I said "Kennel"—the word I use to indicate that he is about to be crated—and then he'd jump into the back of my car and into his dog crate. I'd remove his leash. He'd lie down quietly while I drove to a nearby field.

When I arrived at the field, I'd open the tailgate and his crate, and put his leash back on. Jake would wait until I'd say "Okay," at which time he'd jump out of the car. Then we'd walk onto the field together, with Jake heeling beside me. I'd tell him to sit and I'd take off his leash. We'd walk another forty to fifty feet with Jake heeling correctly. Then and only then would I say "Okay, hi on"—an old British term used to tell dogs to go. And off he'd roar.

The reason I didn't release Jake when I removed his leash is this—I didn't want him to be conditioned to run when he heard the click of the leash. Many owners unconsciously do this. They undermine their ability to command the dog verbally. It may seem a small matter, but when hundreds, even thousands of clicks condition the dog to run, you have lost a vital bit of your control.

Does the schedule I had Jake on seem overly rigid? It isn't. Your pup should be fully capable of doing all of these commands by five months. I'm doing what every owner does when he takes a dog for a walk, except I'm adding a dash of structure. It's not difficult to do; it just requires getting you and your pup into a routine. The more you do it, the easier and better it becomes.

You should continue to exercise your pup every day. Consult with your vet and your breeder as to the proper amount. Jake got a minimum of thirty minutes every morning, rain, sleet, or snow, and I always took him out *before* breakfast. Remember never to feed your dog and then take him out for exercise—it may make him sick. Far more seriously, he could get "stomach torsion," a life-endangering condition caused by the stomach twisting. (You should ask your veterinarian to explain this condition.)

During the four-to-six-month period you have a wonderful opportunity to introduce your puppy to the real world. This is vital to your dog's development because he should learn that the world can be a friendly and interesting place. This reduces the possibility of aggression problems that occur when dogs think the world is hostile. At the same time, it helps you develop control over the pup in a variety of situations. So let him start meeting different people and going to different places.

When Jake was four months old I'd take him to Harvard Square, in Cambridge, Massachusetts. The Square is a very busy area, populated by Harvard and MIT students and people from all around the world. As Jake and I strolled at heel through the Square we'd be stopped by many folks who wanted to pet my baby Lab. I'd tell Jake "Sit" and I'd put my left foot on his leash, making it short enough that Jake couldn't jump on anyone even if he tried. Jake always had a great time meeting so many friendly people.

By the time Jake was five months old he was taking weekend trips with Mary and me on our sailboat *Morning Star*. We'd sail to Martha's Vineyard and anchor in Vineyard Haven. Every morning I'd take Jake ashore so he could eliminate, with my trusty plastic bag with me for clean-up duty. Then we'd head for Jake's favorite place—the Black Dog Bakery! I'd have a breakfast of coffee and croissants while Jake would lie down beside me. The island people were as nice as those in Harvard Square, stopping to chat with me and to play with Jake.

Although I want you to expose your pup to the real world, don't let strangers play with your dog by pounding him on his rib cage. Tell them to knock it off. Don't be shy with strangers. They'll disrupt all the hard work you are putting into developing a good relationship with your pup.

If you follow what I've said, by the end of six months your pup should be housetrained and should be able to do the simple structures of sit, stay, down, come when called, and heel. You should be the leader in the relationship. If you have accomplished all of this, then you will have established the basis of a happy and healthy relationship and greatly reduced the possibility of major dog problems.

CHAPTER

13

Older Dogs

FINDING a good companion in an older dog can be a risky adventure.

Roberta Miller discovered that when she brought home a two-year-old malamute named Jodi who had been owned by a couple with a drug problem. This couple had beaten the dog badly, breaking several ribs. Roberta was very taken with Jodi and wanted to give her the love she so desperately needed.

But Jodi proved difficult to handle. The first time Roberta picked up a broom to sweep the kitchen floor, Jodi ran under the table and literally placed her paws over her head for protection! Whenever friends came over Jodi would scamper out of the room and hide. And no one besides Roberta could come near Jodi without the dog shaking uncontrollably.

I worked with Jodi for a number of weeks using the basic commands to gain control over the dog and to convince her that her new home was safe and secure. With a lot of patience, love, and discipline Jodi became a happy dog again and a wonderful companion to Roberta.

Unfortunately this kind of difficult problem is what I see all too often with older dogs—those over four months of age. There are thousands of dogs at animal shelters, humane agencies, dog pounds, and in homes where they're no longer wanted or loved. Unless they're claimed, they'll have to be put to death. In 1986 the Massachusetts Society for the Prevention of Cruelty to Animals euthanized more than 30,000 dogs!

Many of these dogs are the product of a family who "just wanted to have one litter," or who wished their child to see the wonder of birth. Such thoughtless breeding ultimately ends in tragedy.

What's a shelter dog like? The National Animal Control Association in 1981 conducted a survey which revealed that two thirds of the dogs adopted have been acquired free. Of the owners who gave up their dog, 28 percent did it because of changes in their life-style, 26 percent because their dog had behavioral problems, and 12 percent because care of their dog became too much. These owners are dumping their dog on society.

With this in mind, if you still want to acquire an older dog, then you have my admiration—as well as a lot of advice. First, look beyond those loving eyes and *never feel sorry for that dog*. Now most owners who take a dog from a shelter *do* feel sorry for that dog. It's natural. But it's a dangerous attitude to have because it not only will subvert your ability to pick a good dog but it will undermine the possibility of establishing a healthy relationship with your new canine friend.

When you go looking for that new dog here are a few suggestions. As I recommended in the chapter on puppies, whenever you are going to buy a dog you must think about your life-style and needs before you do anything. After you've done that, talk to the shelter manager or shelter personnel. They know dogs and particularly those at their shelter. Be honest. Tell them what you have in mind for a dog, and then explain to them about your children, your experience with dogs, what expectations you have for the dog, your daily schedule, and if you have another dog, how they might get along. They'll be eager to help. But you must realize that shelters often don't know much about the pup's background.

You therefore should be careful to get as much information from them based on their experience with Bozo. You should ask them:

- How much the dog eats
- How much grooming is involved
- How much daily exercise is necessary
- How the dog is with people and with other dogs
- What his medical history is

Most of all, be observant. If there is something about the dog that disturbs you, ask. For example, if you see some redness on the dog's skin find out about it. Bozo may have a chronic skin allergy that will cost you a lot of money to deal with after you've taken him home.

If you get poor answers to any of your questions or a bad feeling about the shelter, just leave.

After you've made your choice I want you to remember that a mutt is as much of a responsibility for you as an eight-hundred-dollar show quality, pure-bred animal. His capacity for love is not diminished in any way because there's mongrel blood flowing through his veins.

Structuring should begin within three days after bringing your dog home. This reduces the chance of your over-indulging the dog and acts as a confidence builder for the new arrival. For the same reasons, you should also be setting limits right away, letting him know clearly what is expected of him, and that when he does the correct thing, he gets rewarded. Your dog may respond quite well to structure and setting of limits, or he may not. It's possible that his previous owner or situation conditioned him not to respond to people. You'll have to decide how much work you need to do based on how he acts.

It's best to think of your new dog as an adolescent foster child. When that child is placed with foster parents, he or she needs two things from the outset—affection and discipline. Let him know precisely where he is in the pecking order of your home. He'll become a much better companion for you. But be restrained in your corrections during the first few days or the dog will wish he were back at the shelter. The three watchwords during this initial time are *patience, patience, patience.*

The first two to three weeks you have your dog can be crucial for your relationship. Bozo may be fairly calm during this period of time, since he's adapting to a new environment and making his observations of his new owner—he's trying to figure out whether you're a leader, a wimp, or an overindulgent attendant. Within a month the dog's real personality will emerge. So keep structuring and setting limits. Be sure to get the whole family involved with these activities so as not to let him try to become second-in-command.

I also want you to observe the dog carefully during the first couple of weeks he's at home. Watch him as much as he's watching you. Determine what commands he already knows. Find out if he's been an indoor dog or outdoor dog (if he's got good muscle tone and rough pads on the bottom of his feet then he's been outdoors a lot). Take time to see if he's got a housesoiling problem (he might be peeing because he's not used to your home). See if he has any phobias, such as loud noises. All this is information you can use to head off or control problems and to begin playful activities with the dog.

One week after you bring Bozo home you should make an appointment with a vet. His or her examination can provide you with medical explanations for any problems you've observed. The vet will also help you set up a good exercise schedule and a proper diet.

My final words of advice come down to using common sense with an older dog. They can make wonderful pets, but also much trouble can lurk behind those big, brown eyes. To quote Sergeant Phil Esterhaus's warning to the cops on *Hill Street Blues*, "Hey, let's be careful out there."

CHAPTER 14

Children

MY next-door neighbors Evans and Holly have a two-year-old boy named Sam and a dog named Cameo (see picture on page 162). Sam and Cameo have a wonderful relationship. When I look out my kitchen window, I can see them playing happily in their backyard.

Several weeks after I brought Jake home, my neighbors came over to see the new arrival. As soon as Sam spotted Jake he walked over and touched Jake on the nose, not harmfully, but as if he were pushing a black elevator button. Then he threw his arms around Jake and gave him a big kiss. Evans, Holly, and I laughed heartily. Jake, however, had had enough, and broke free from Sam's embrace, taking off for my backyard, with Sam in hot pursuit.

Ever since, Sam and Jake have been great friends, with Cameo joining them for ball throwing contests and catch-me-if-you-can romps across both backyards.

What I see out my kitchen window is almost an ideal child-dog relationship. It works so well because Cameo and Jake both love children and Evans and Holly had carefully thought about how to introduce Cameo to their son. In addition, I had taken Jake near other people and some children before he ran into his backyard buddy. Unfortunately,

My friends Sam and Cameo.

most of my housecalls reveal a sharply different picture. In many cases, parents have had a dog in the family for a number of years before deciding to have a baby, often treating Bozo as a surrogate child. These owners just assume that baby and Bozo will get along. Within a few days after the arrival of their bundle of joy they find out how wrong they can be. Frequently the dog will start growling and showing teeth when the baby's brought in the room. Frightened, the parents call me, desperate to understand why their beloved canine companion won't love their child.

The first thing I explain to parents is that the dog must make a positive association with the baby. If he doesn't make a positive one, he'll make a negative one. The parents have to realize that when they bring the baby home he's invading the dog's territory. Bozo isn't naturally inclined to love the child. In fact, what usually happens is this: The mother brings her child over to Bozo and he growls. The father dashes over, whacks the dog, and drags him outside. Time passes and the baby is put to sleep. The owners, feeling guilty, let Bozo back in and give him a few loving pats and coo affectionate words. Several hours later the baby wakes up, is brought out, Bozo growls, and out he goes.

What has the dog learned? When the baby's in the room, the dog gets punished. When the baby is gone, he gets affection, or at least, everything is back to normal, like before that rotten little kid invaded Bozo's home.

Punishment is not the answer to making Bozo love your child. What you have to do is *switch* the dog out of his initial negative reaction to a positive association. Here's how to do that. When you bring the baby into a room take a ball with you. As Bozo comes near you and your child, throw the ball, have Bozo retrieve it, pat him when he comes back with it and say enthusiastically, "Good dog, good dog." Do this up to ten times, or as many as you enjoy. What's the dog learning now? Whenever the new arrival comes in, I'm going to have fun.

You can continue this positive association in another simple way. When it comes time for feeding the baby, have Bozo lie down quietly beside you. If you have to, put his leash on and hold it down with your foot. While you feed the baby, just reach over and pat the dog and say "Good dog."

You can think of numerous other instances when you can reward Bozo for being good around the baby. But remember you must keep positive programming going until Bozo and child have firmly established a healthy relationship. A short while ago I visited with Nancy and Bob Ferraro, whose dog, Ralph, a German shepherd was growling at the new baby. They began my program and the dog responded very well to it. But Nancy fell sick and her mother came from Chattanooga, Tennessee, to help out with the child. Unfortunately, the grandmother was nervous around dogs and my program fell by the wayside as the dog was put in the yard every time the baby was brought out. Ten days after the grandmother arrived Bob called me to tell me his dog was growling again and wanted to know what to do. There was only one answer—put the grandmother on the first plane home and resume the program.

After the initial introduction of the child, parents usually have a breather until the seventh month. At that time, the baby becomes mobile—thanks to the invention of the walker. Now the child can race around the floor chasing the dog. Of course, the dog feels threatened and may turn, after enough threats, and bite the child. The most obvious solution is to stop the child from chasing Bozo. But since parents can't watch their child every second I recommend a healthy dose of positive association. Here's what I did with the O'Shea family. I asked Bob and Betty and the child's maternal grandparents (who frequently babysat) to bring the baby and their seven-year-old Airedale named Daddy Wags into the living room. I then had each adult stand in a corner of the room, with Betty holding her child. I had Betty call Daddy Wags and as he approached her everyone shouted out "Good dog." If Daddy Wags headed toward any of the other adults I had them ignore him. I then repeated the exercise with each adult.

What was I trying to achieve with this curious game? I wanted the dog to understand that good things happen to him when he approached the baby and acted in a pleasant manner. This exercise worked so well that the grandmother called me a while ago to tell me that dog and child are now sleeping together on the floor.

The problems I've been describing all involve situations where the dog is already in the household. What happens when parents decide to get a dog for a child? The first mistake most parents make is not investigating the proper breed of dog for children. There are breeds that are genetically predisposed toward a better temperament with children than others. Daniel F. Tortora's book, *The Right Dog for You* (Simon and Schuster, 1980), is a fine guide for selecting the right dog for your child, although I disagree with him on his assessment of the English springer spaniel and the golden retriever. I caution parents about these two breeds, which, in my experience, are having more than their share of temperament problems and will continue to do so for some time. Less than responsible breeding is the cause of this problem. If you really want to buy these breeds for your child, please investigate the breeder and his or her line as much as possible before the purchase.

I feel strongly that parents should wait until the child reaches the age of five before picking a dog. Up to that age the child tends to view the dog as a playmate, a moveable stuffed toy. He has a very limited understanding of what a dog is. After five the child can reasonably be expected to take responsibility for the dog's behavior. He's capable of doing the basic commands with the dog, once the dog has been taught them by the owner. Doing structuring will improve the bond between child and dog, as will walking, feeding, and brushing the pup. At first parents should supervise these activities, making sure the child doesn't try to boss the dog around.

If *any* aggression (growling or biting) is shown toward the child, consult immediately with either a vet or a trainer. I'm very strict about this situation. All possible steps should be tried to deal with the dog's aggressive behavior (see Chapter Six). But when these have been exhausted, parents must realize that the child's safety comes first and the dog should probably be put to sleep.

Having walked through all the problems associated with children and dogs, let me close with a story of how special these relationships can be. A woman named Jane Ambash called me to work with a young puppy named Molly. Jane's daughter, Lizzie, was severely autistic and Jane was afraid that Molly might bite her child, because the pup was mouthy. But the dog had already accomplished a miracle. When Lizzie and Molly had first spotted each other, Lizzie got up and took three steps toward the pup. Jane was astonished, because the physical therapist who worked with Lizzie said the child was more than a year away from walking. However, since that fateful meeting, Lizzie had only limited exposure to Molly because of Jane's fear the dog would bite.

We gathered in the living room—me, the therapist, and

Lizzie—to await Molly's arrival. Lizzie—a pretty little girl with dark eyes and hair—sat on a big foam cushion. Jane came in from a back room with Molly. As soon as Jane put the pup down she raced into the center of the living room, her eyes dancing and her tail wagging. Molly came over to Lizzy as she sat on the cushion and put her mouth on Lizzy's arm. We just left them alone. After several minutes Molly got tired and started to lick Lizzy's face. Jane nervously said, "Ray, should we break them up?" I told Jane to wait so we could see what would happen.

After a few minutes child and dog started to play with each other, first roughly and then more gently. A few minutes more went by and slowly Lizzie and Molly embraced, resting peacefully next to each other. Jane went to pick up her daughter. She hugged both child and dog.

Three years have passed and Lizzie continues to make progress. She and Molly are inseparable companions and never have I seen more love between a child and a dog.

Five is the best age for children to start enjoying a dog.

CHAPTER
15

Just for the Fun of It

MANY evenings I spend my time lecturing at dog clubs and veterinary clinics. Recently, in a small town in Vermont, after I'd gone through the wrong ways people handle their dogs, the kinds of problems I see all the time, and the methods for dealing with these problems, a young man raised his hand and asked me this question, "Mr. McSoley, for the last hour I've heard you say, 'Don't do this, don't that, and if you have troubles do this, this, and this.' How the hell am I going to have fun with my dog?" His question was an excellent one.

As in my lectures, I've spent the previous chapters telling you what's wrong with your dog and how to fix it. But here's the final rule I'll leave with you: HAVE FUN WITH YOUR DOG. It's really the only reason to have a dog. I don't think any other animal can give you as much pleasure and satisfaction as man's best friend.

The best way to keep your relationship pleasurable is to challenge your dog. Keep him on his toes by having to deal with new experiences. Local breed clubs or dog training clubs are the ideal place to work with Bozo. If you have a mongrel, join up. Don't feel like a second-class dog owner at a club if you don't have a purebred dog. You can't compete

Jake and me having some fun retrieving...

. . .good dog, Jake, good dog.

in obedience trials sanctioned or licensed by the American Kennel Club, but what do you care? You can still take part in fun matches. Your dog doesn't know the difference, so why should you be concerned.

There are many other competitions for your dog. Tracking tests are just one example. The dog, over a prescribed course, tracks a target by scent, an excellent confidence builder for the animal. Many clubs now hold terrier digs for that class of dog. Herding tests and water trials are another possibility. If you own a Newfoundland, investigate the "Newfy" water trials. There are clubs holding herding competition for the herding breeds and dachshund races are popular at some clubs. As you progress upward in competition, they become progressively more difficult, challenging, and fun.

Find out what is available for you and your dog. There are lots of people in those clubs who'll show you the ropes when you get started. The best part is that you'll be involved with people who have something in common—they really enjoy their dogs. That will only enhance your pleasure.

Jake and I just took part in a retriever field trial. Jake

did very well and his brother Bud even better—he placed first!

I also want you to keep the fun going at home, even when you're doing the basic structuring commands. When you get up for a beer, tell Bozo to stay. When you come back, pat him and tell him what a good dog he is. If you're out walking your dog at heel, stop and give him a good hug every once in a while for doing a good job.

Finally, find some activity you can enjoy together. The most fun Jake and I have is doing what he was bred to do —retrieve. We retrieve *every day* even if it is for no more than three minutes, or two retrieves. I also take him either for a thirty-minute run every morning or, if the snow in my hometown of Westwood is too deep, I walk him for two miles around our local pond. We walk at heel and we discuss the nation's business, current events, and some of the dog problems I'll be facing that day. I do at least one short, five-minute structure session with Jake daily.

Well that's about all the advice I've got to give. It's time for me to go. I hope the stories I've told you and the ideas I've presented enhance your relationship with your canine friend and help solve whatever problems you might be having. Right now Jake is wagging his tail, telling me to get ready for our walk. It's time to stop being an author and go out and have some fun with my friend.

Appendix

I've enclosed the form that I give my clients when I visit them. Fill it out and it will help you deal with your dog problems.

RAY McSOLEY'S DOG PROBLEM-SOLVING NOTEBOOK

I. General Information

A. Dog's name: _____

B. Dog's age: _____

C. Dog's sex: _____

D. Dog's breed: _____

II. Dog's Basic History

A. How old was he/she when obtained? _____

B. Who was he/she obtained from? _____

C. Number in the litter? _____

D. Why did you pick your dog? _____

E. Why did you select this particular breed? _____

_____

F. Is this your first dog? _____
G. Briefly describe your dog's medical history. _____

_____

III. Problem Behavior Information

A. Briefly describe your dog's problem. _____

_____

_____

_____

B. When did the problem begin? _____

_____

C. Has the problem increased/decreased since? _____

D. What steps have you taken to correct the problem? ___

_____

_____

E. Is there a particular time of day when the behavior is
most likely to occur? _____

_____

IV. Daily life of your dog

Describe a typical daily schedule for your dog from the time
he/she wakes up to the time he/she retires. _____

_____

_____

_____

_____

_____

_____

Does the weekend schedule change? If so, how? _____
_____
_____
_____

V. Your dog and obedience

A. How do you correct your dog for misbehaviors? _____
_____

B. Are these corrections effective? _____
_____

C. Has your dog ever growled at you? _____
_____

D. Can you take bones and other objects away from your dog? _____
_____

E. Have you taken your dog to obedience school? _____
F. Describe how your dog did at obedience school. _____
_____

G. Did other family members go? _____
H. How would you rate your dog on obedience?
   Good/Fair/Poor
_____

I. Who is the chief disciplinarian in your house? _____
_____

J. Does your dog get angry at you when disciplined? _____
If yes, how does he/she express it? _____

VI. Your dog's diet

A. What does your dog eat? _____
_____

B. When is he/she fed? _____
C. Does he/she have a very good/good/poor appetite? ____
_____

D. Does he/she get treats? _____ Table scraps? ____

E. Does he/she have water available at all times? _____

F. Is your dog underweight/overweight? _____

VII. Your dog's activities

A. Does your dog get sufficient exercise? _____

B. How much time per day is he/she outdoors? _____

C. Does he/she run free _____ On a run? _____

In a fenced-in yard _____ If yes, type of fencing. ___

_____

D. Does he/she bark outside? _____ Is it a problem?

_____

VIII. Your dog and others

A. Does your dog like/tolerate/dislike strangers? _____

_____

B. Does your dog like/tolerate/dislike your friends
and relatives? _____

_____

C. Does your dog like/tolerate/dislike children? _____

_____

D. Does your dog like/tolerate/dislike other dogs? _____

_____

E. What is your dog's behavior in your car? _____

_____

F. What is your dog's behavior at gas stations? _____

_____

G. What is your dog's behavior at toll booths? _____

_____

H. What is your dog's behavior at the groomer's? _____

_____

I. What is your dog's behavior at the vet's? _____

_____